Green Light Selling

By

Don Aspromonte

TABLE OF CONTENTS

FORWARD

Diligence, determination, and persistence are required for significant successes. Fear, self-consciousness, and lack of preparation often prevent good people from achieving worthwhile goals.

This exciting book contains proven, practical techniques that can help persistent salespeople stay on track as they move to toward their life successes. You will deepen your understanding regarding how top sales performers think and behave. The reader will learn the same skills top performers use to engage the customer in the problem solving process.

The sales model presented goes well beyond preparing you for merely "handling objections." Unlike other material, Green Light Selling highlights the importance of developing an on-going relationship with the customer. Becoming proficient at the specific language and interpersonal skills presented will take the fear out of selling.

This book will teach you how to help your customer think more creatively - so they have a sense of 'ownership' about the solutions you create together. These techniques go a long way toward developing your confidence and cementing a real partnership between the seller and the buyer.

Who will benefit from this book? Certainly professional salespeople will find specific techniques for improving their earnings. Because this book is about powerful communication techniques, managers, trainers, and negotiators will also find the concepts presented very useful.

We recommend this book to anyone who needs to communicate ideas effectively. Mastering these skills will help you be of service to others while making sure you remain ethical. If you really want to become a master communicator, this book will be an important step forward for you!

Introduction

Natural born salespeople are not really born that way. They simply learned (usually by stumbling upon it) a wonderful sales structure that works well, and then they repeated it over and over. Now, with Green Light Selling, you can too! After 10 years researching the most successful salespeople (producing 100%-300% of their quotas every year), we found the secret that great salespeople all share. Just as the melting of snow from the mountain peaks reveals the strong rugged rocks beneath, we discovered the actual structure that makes the Sales Masters successful.

- Green Light Selling techniques help you radically increase your sales quotas and more!

In business, NOTHING HAPPENS UNTIL SOMEONE MAKES A SALE. This book is about bringing in your sales, consistently year-in-year-out by using professional communication skills and the latest linguistic techniques modeled from TOP SALES PERFORMERS. Much like Napoleon Hill (author of Think and Grow Rich), we studied the TOP SALES PERFORMERS from many fields; what they do and exactly **HOW** they do it. By stripping the verbiage from successful sales interactions, we discovered that there is a common structure holding a successful sale together. This book teaches you step by step HOW to use the process and be wildly successful.

Imagine for a moment, driving in the city down a one-way street. About every other block there is a stop light. If you don't time your approach correctly, you will get caught at a red light. Once you hit that first red light, you will have to stop at all the red lights the whole way across town. But, if you understand the structure of how the lights have their timing set, you can have Green Lights all the way home. You will get where you want to go, faster and more pleasantly. Likewise, with **Green Light Selling** you get your sales faster and more pleasantly. You hit GREEN LIGHTS the whole way.

You can grasp the **Green Light Selling** model concepts in a relatively short time. The process is packaged into small, learnable chunks to allow you to easily integrate the steps and techniques into your own personal style. Many readers improved their capabilities in some areas immediately and their overall competency in weeks.

Others have had startling overnight results by using just one or two of the techniques outlined in this book.

The *top performers* we studied enjoy their work, have high ethical standards, family lives, and traditional values. After 20 years in the sales field, many of these individuals are still performing today and have not suffered from the many stress diseases that others in the field fall prey to. They look good, feel good, and play hard.

The 5-step Green Light Selling model in this book adapts easily to fit your own personal style and allows you to emulate these Sales Masters. With practice, you will be applying this model with the same ease as other top performers.

Nothing In This Sales Model Was Invented - It Was All Discovered

This universal selling structure has been tested by thousands of real sales people, selling real products and services in highly competitive markets, to determine its workability. It is now possible to sell almost any product or service from this one basic format. With the **Green Light Selling** model you need only follow the structure and vary the product information to fit your particular product or service.

The question is, "What kind of a salesperson do you want to be?" **If you want to close 75% to 85% of your viable prospects in half the selling time, this method is for you!** There are many needs in the marketplace. With the sales model presented here, you will be able to supply those needs for people in a way that meets the customer's goals while also meeting yours. As Zig Ziglar said, "You can get everything in life you want if you help enough other people get what they want."

Using the techniques outlined in this book will help you make the sales you want and avoid the dead ends you've had in the past. In life, there are many opportunities for you to supply the needs of others and for your efforts be properly compensated - even richly rewarded. Let **Green Light Selling** eliminate many of the roadblocks for you!

1. OVERVIEW: GREENLIGHT MODEL

'How do you do it, Don?' Her face wore the same perplexed expression I had seen on the faces of countless rookie sales people. 'When you do it, it seems so easy.'

Behind my back they said I was a natural born salesman. I knew I wasn't. I leaned just like everyone else. Now, after over 20 years of selling, I seriously considered the question. How could I teach others how to make the sale time after time?

Neurolinquistic Programming (NLP) training was the key that I needed to make this communication technology available to anyone who wants to learn to sell professionally. NLP gave me the tools to model great salespeople and sales managers and understand what was actually causing them to be successful. NLP modeling allowed me to sort out the "differences that made a difference" between their winning behaviors and ordinary sales people's occasionally successful behaviors. The top people are consistently the 20% of the sales force that brings in 80% of the business. The 80% of the sales force that brings in 20% of the business are typically using ordinary social skills that force them to work hard for little reward. As a mentor of mine once observed, "Even a blind monkey finds an occasional banana". Modeling is necessary to separate personality (which is interesting, but not necessarily important to sales success) from behaviors and responses that are critically important to sales success.

NLP was the key to training methods that allow the transfer of these discoveries to anyone willing to experience the discomfort of learning new behaviors. Learning concepts and catch phrases in seminar situations is much different from developing new behaviors that can actually change the results of the next sales interaction. There are wonderful speakers, books and tapes with absolutely valid concepts and ideas available to everyone who wants to take the time to study them. But until these ideas are embedded in your automatic behaviors, they will not change your daily sales results. NLP training methods allow people to change their responses immediately and permanently.

For example, most sales people are great "talkers" and marginal "listeners". Most salespeople know that they need to be better listeners. Some have even taken "Effective Listening Skills" courses. Those skills do not necessarily become an integral part of their sales activity. NLP training techniques make it possible for a naturally poor listener to become a great listener in their next sales call. Not only do they actually listen to the prospect, the prospect is *aware* that they are really listening. Every skill that is necessary to become a top sales performer is represented in the Green Light Selling model, and can be delivered with NLP training techniques.

WHAT MAKES A SALE

The world is full of prospective buyers of your goods and services. But what *makes* the sale? Once I began picking apart what successful salespersons did, I realized it isn't necessary to teach more about products in order to show others how they can sell better. The *key is in the structure*: How you present the information and the order it is presented in. All salespeople can benefit from a fuller understanding of the structure of selling. **Green Light Selling** helps you gain insights into this concept of structure. Whether you have been a salesperson for a long time or you are just getting into the field, the **Green Light Selling** model presented here has the potential to revolutionize your style of selling much as the invention of the automobile revolutionized transportation.

First, you must change how you approach the very basics of how you sell. Changing your focus on *what happens during a sale* causes a change in your perception and subsequently an improvement in your sales abilities. Focusing on the structure of the sales situation automatically makes you more effective. All people who enter the field of sales have probably at some time riveted their attention to product description. They may have learned the "buzz words' and "trade secrets," and then used them to present their product or service in a way that sometimes did and sometimes did not result in a sale. Using the times that were successful as a basis, they then decided which method worked for them and then continued to do more of that.

In fact, less successful salespeople usually use that same method over and over whether it fits their current customer or not. That is how they lose sales. For example, they may have decided that what worked was presenting a good demonstration. This is effective for about 25% of the population. Or, they may have decided that the best technique was telling everything about their product. This works for about 20 % of the people. That leaves 75 % and 80 % of the time when their selected approaches lead to dead ends. No sales. Those are pretty high odds in favor of failing!

No single sales gambit or technique works on all prospects! Salespeople tend to repeat what they have learned whether it accomplishes what they want or not. The difference between successful salespeople and the rest is in what they repeat. *Successful salespeople don't just repeat techniques, they follow a winning sales structure. There is one structural model that usually works for everyone. That structure is the **Green Light Selling** model and following it will work for you too!*

THE STRENGTH OF STRUCTURE

There is a natural order to the way an objective can be accomplished. Consider how a house is built. The basic structure begins with a foundation, moves to a floor and walls, and eventually ends with a roof. There must be adequate support at the base for the roof to balance properly. Leaving out any of the required steps in the building process can make the whole building unstable. Following all the steps results in a solid building that lasts for many years. Once the house is finished, the inside may be filled with a variety of furnishings which reflect the owner's individual style. Wallpaper, paint, and accents make the structure warm and personal inside. A soundly built structure remains intact even though the contents may change many times during its lifetime.

In the same way, an effective structure for selling follows a natural directional flow from entrance to exit and creates a strong selling foundation. Leaving out even a single step can weaken the structure and jeopardize your chances for making a sale. The **Green Light Selling** model is a blueprint for a properly built selling structure with an entrance, five steps, and an exit.

As you carefully follow these steps in-your daily selling, you will find that most of your opportunities will result in sales. Just as the basic structure of a house remains the same, the **Green Light Selling** model remains the same even though the words or contents vary from person to person and product to product.

Understanding the **Green Light Selling** structure may be difficult or easy, depending on your natural way of thinking. If you do not ordinarily pay attention to structure, you will find this book especially helpful.

AMATEUR VERSUS PROFESSIONAL

"Amateurs hope. Professionals work."
Garson Kanin

In any field, there is a noticeable difference between practiced amateurs and professionals. Amateurs may begin their approach just as professionals by doing Step 1. Both may continue following Step 2. After Step 3, a little irrelevancy may creep in as a prospect mentions a recent trip to Hawaii. The amateur may respond by mentioning a Hawaiian trip he also took. The two may continue talking about vacations for a while. One topic leads to another and soon the sales amateur feels as if they are good friends. In fact, an amateur may consider they are such good buddies that at this point he attempts to a close his sale. The prospect will then usually back off quickly and say, "I need to think about this a little more. Say, can we get together some other time?" The amateur's common mistake is either forgetting a step or thinking the rest of the steps are unnecessary.

Know Where You Are

It is imperative to know where you are in the selling process at all times. When using the **Green Light Selling** model, you must start at the beginning with your Entrance and follow ALL 5 Steps to your Exit at the end of your transaction. No matter how many side excursions you take, you MUST always come back to the step you were on when you left or you will lose the sale! If you attempt to build your roof before your walls and foundation are complete, you'll end up having to tunnel your way out in the dark. Remember, Entrance, ALL 5 Steps, then Exit. When you finally reach your Exit, you'll know you have covered all the relevant material in a specific order.

- **Here lies the difference between the Amateur and the Professional. A PROFESSIONAL NEVER SKFPS STEPS!!**

We suggest that you learn the 5 simple steps of the **Green Light Selling** process. Make sure you always use each one in the proper order. If you decide later to add steps or rearrange them, you have a way to evaluate the effectiveness of your changes and whether or not the changes are useful to you. Throughout the course of this book, you are introduced to the **Green Light Selling** model one step at a time. Practice each step until you are totally comfortable with it and have assimilated the step into your personal style. Now, let's touch on the whole model briefly before you learn each step in depth.

THE GREEN LIGHT SELLING STRUCTURE

An Entrance - Five Steps - And An Exit

Entrance.
The **Green Light Selling** model begins with an ENTRANCE. In fact, your Entrance is almost a complete sales process all by itself. This is how the tone of the sales relationship gets established. During the first few moments of an interaction, you begin to teach people how to treat you. For example, you should say "Hello" and then wait for a reply. *If you do not wait for a reply and just rush on to begin to tell your story, you are teaching the other person that they do not need to respond to you.* If the prospect formulates this habit in those first moments, you will continue to have non-responsive problems with your customer from then on.

> *"To be persuasive, we must be believable.*
> *To be believable, we must be credible.*
> *To be credible, we must be truthful."*
> -Edward R. Murrow

The Entrance focuses on the relationship that you must develop to keep your customer. In Chapters 2 and 3, you learn specific language patterns that insure everything you do from the first moment communicates that you fully expect "a symmetrical relationship" - where both the salesman and the prospect give and take. You learn the importance of giving some information and then asking for information. You will also see why you should not get too far ahead in your giving. Chapter 3 offers additional pointers on how important it is to focus on the end-point (Exit) of your sale from the very beginning (Entrance). Just like a swimmer, once you are in the sales waters you must keep your eye on the shore (Exit). Otherwise you lose your way and sink!

Step 1. Rapport Frames.

Rapport could be described as a "deep abiding interest and communication" between two or more people. Without rapport, the sale is destined for failure. During Step 1, three important levels of rapport are established. You learn why prospects sometimes drop out of rapport with you and how to re-establish a positive working relationship. The concept of three distinctly different levels of rapport has been very helpful to individuals wanting to enhance their communication techniques. The rapport skills outlined in Chapter 4 help you refine your sales interactions for efficiency, effectiveness, and a profitable, long-term association.

Step 2. Buying Procedure - Backtrack / Conditional Close.

Chapter 5 details information on Backtracking and Conditional Close techniques. Backtracking is similar to the familiar technique used in other sales trainings called "restate the objection." You learn some modem linguistic enhancements that makes the **Green Light Selling** concept work even more elegantly and with incredible precision.

The Conditional Close is similar to J. Douglas Edward's technique called the "Sharp Angle Close," but the Green Light Selling technique is much softer and can be used more often without losing rapport. It also demonstrates that you are taking the customer's needs seriously. Of course, you learn specific language patterns as well as the underlying structure of this excellent information gathering process.

In Chapter 6, you learn how to uncover your customer's Buying Procedure - the method(s) your prospect has used before to make their buying decisions. If you ever experienced a sales opportunity "go sour" after you'd done 90 % of the work, you will really love these techniques. You learn how top sales people keep complex sales campaigns on track - all the way to the close.

Step 3. Needs Elicitation.

In this step, the prospect tells you their needs and requirements. You will be able to comfortably listen to the prospect's 'wish list.' Because of the unique integrated nature of the **Green Light Selling** model, even outrageous customer requirements (that are light years from reality) can usually be handled gracefully. Specific instructions for learning this step are offered in Chapter 7.

Step 4. Get To Intent/Translate.

After the prospects have offered their 'wish lists," the next step is to make sure you understand the function of each specified item. Even seasoned salespeople make serious mistakes at this point. For example, if a product weakness has come to your attention recently (in the form of an objection), that weakness will stand out in your mind. If a prospect begins to suggest requirements in this area of weakness, you may over-respond and jump to erroneous conclusions. This reaction often leads to defensive behavior that can create unnecessary problems for you.

With the questioning and clarification techniques discussed in detail in Chapter 8, you learn to "translate' the impossible into the 'do-able.' You develop deeper rapport and more appreciation for your customer's real needs. You discover new ways to meet your prospect's needs by following simple and effective linguistic processes.

Step 5. Pivot Point Presentation / Close.

During this step, the prospect's needs are connected to the features of your product or service. In Chapter 9, you find that there are two basic ways to tell the prospect about your product. One way is the most natural and comfortable way to discuss your product - and the least effective. The other way, called the Pivot-Point Presentation, may be more difficult for you, and yet it is much more persuasive to your prospect. You discover how to get the greatest possible mileage out of your product's features with this method. In fact, you can expect to close 75% to 85% of your viable prospects because your product will be presented with more impact.

In Chapter 10, we explore new insights into the closing process. After following the Pivot-Point Presentation process faithfully, you will notice that the "once feared close" is almost automatic and anti-climactic. You learn a proven closing technique to help you succeed with the many different kinds of buyers you encounter throughout your sales career.

Exit.
The Exit can be an important part of the entire process. Too often, skilled salespeople lose future business because of a sloppy exit. Consistently getting closure on each transaction and setting up the potential for future interactions is the hallmark of top sales performers.

GREEN LIGHTS ALL THE WAY
To present the sales model clearly, we have defined each step of the **Green Light Selling** model and each step actually dove tails smoothly into the next. Learning the **Green Light Selling** model requires practice - similar to first learning how to drive a car - but with practice, it becomes automatic. When you first learn to drive, it is necessary to concentrate on each step individually. Once you have mastered each step, you begin to think of the second step and begin implementing it while you are finishing the first step. Eventually, you get so skilled that even while you are shifting into gear, you are also glancing in your rear view mirror, paying attention to the road ahead, and pushing on the gas pedal without skipping a beat.

When you first think of rapport frames (Step I in the Green Light Selling model), you will be aware of your speech and its effect on your prospect. As you gain more expertise in choosing your words and gauging their effect on others, your skills become polished and automatic. For **Green Light Selling** to work, each step in the process needs to be practiced until it becomes natural for you and your style.

> "Don't give up whatever you've trying to do - especially if you're convinced that you're botching it up. Giving up reinforces a sense of incompetence, going on gives you a commitment to success."
> -George Weinberg

Just reading this book will NOT bring you sales success. Practicing the model will. Practice helps you make the sales process flow correctly and helps you recognize when the flow has choked up. For example, going backwards in a conversation to add something you forgot to say creates confusion in the mind of the listener, much as stroking a cat the wrong way creates static electricity.

The natural directional flow of language and processes in the sales structure requires that you start at the beginning and move through all the steps to a successful end EACH AND EVERY TIME. Attempting to back up to cover forgotten ground can be disastrous.

Learning the **Green Light Selling** model and following the 5 specific steps moves you and your prospect from beginning (Entrance) to close (Exit) in an orderly fashion. Before long, your timing clicks in and you are moving through all the intersections with green lights shining for you all the way. The more discipline you put into practicing the **Green Light Selling** model, the sooner you soar with the Sales Masters.

POINTS TO REMEMBER-
1. LEARN THE STEPS
2. NEVER SKIP STEPS
3. PRACTICE YOUR ENTRANCE, ALL FIVE STEPS OF THIS PROCESS, AND YOUR EXIT UNTIL IT AUTOMATICALLY BECOMES NATURAL FOR YOU AND YOUR PERSONAL STYLE

Chapter 2

Words can make or break your career in sales. Your words are your personal sales tools; how you use them is critical to your success. Like a fine craftsperson, you want to use the highest quality tools available. Most of us are aware that words can be used to sway people. Until now however, few people understood how specific words and word combinations can have predictable effects upon the listener. To use the **Green Light Selling** model effectively, you need to be aware of how these words operate and how to use them correctly.

- **This chapter covers words that can cause you problems and shows you how to avoid those problems.**

What you are about to learn may seem simple to you. If so, splendid! You will pick up these skills easily. Despite their apparent simplicity, DO READ AND PRACTICE the material. By using the wrong combination of words, you can inadvertently sabotage your own sales points very quickly. It happens everyday.

"Those who speak 'straight from the shoulder' should try it from a little higher UP-"
- Anonymous

The following section covers words you use everyday and how they can affect your communication in ways you might have never considered. When you change how you use these words, you will be amazed at what a difference something so simple as changing a word tense can make throughout all of your sales encounters.

DELETE WORDS WITH NEGATIVE IMPACT
There are three words that often have negative impact at the unconscious level of the mind. These words are why, try, and but. You probably use these words every day without noticing the unwanted response they cause. However, you will be amazed what a difference subtle changes can make. Your interactions with prospective clients have more impact if you consciously delete the use of these words from your interactions. Before you know it, you will automatically be saying all the right things.

Delete WHY - Substitute HOW, WHEN, WHO, WHERE WHICH
The word WHY has a peculiar effect on most people. Its use causes

confusion in the mind of the person it is directed toward. If you ask, "Why?" the other person usually does not understand what you want and is likely to feel accused and react defensively. As a result, the customer will most likely answer the WHY question with rhetoric which justifies their position, rather than providing you with any useful content. This is especially detrimental if what you wanted to accomplish was to get more information. To clarify your question, substitute one of these words: *how, when, who, where, or which.*

Rather than saying.
"Why did you do that?"
Substitute WHY with:
"Can you tell me **how** you arrived at that conclusion?"

"**Wha**t motivated you to do that?"

"Just **when** did you arrive at that conclusion?"

"**Where** did you get the background to decide so quickly?"

"I know you use special techniques in making your decisions. **Which** one did you use today?"

Using these kinds of substitutions usually gets you a higher quality, informational answer that offers the specifics your question originally intended.

Delete TRY - Substitute DO
TRY is one of those words that actually gives two answers to a question. An example of this is when you invite someone over for dinner and they say, "I'll try." The two answers are:
"I believe I should come in order to honor our relationship, but I'm not coming."
The inference of **TRY** is the word fail. Test this for yourself. Make up a few ordinary sentences in which you would use the word try, and then substitute the word fail in its place. In most cases, the sentence conveys the same negative message either way. To remedy this, get in the habit of substituting the word **DO for TRY.**

You will probably find that after inserting the word **DO**, the MEANING of the sentence remains the same but the meaning switches into a positive frame.

Instead of: "That is what I will **TRY** today."

Substitute: "That is what I will **DO** today."

The purpose of salesmanship is to get people to do something. It is not your job, as a general rule, to suggest to people that they fail (by using the word TRY).
Whenever you begin to say the word **TRY** - ask yourself what you really want them to **DO**, and say that instead. For example, if you are about to say, "I would like to try to convince you that my company can serve you very well," just hesitate for a moment. Think about what you want to do instead, and then say, "I would like to convince you that my company can serve you very well.'

Of course you may have to use several sentences to avoid the word **TRY** to still convey your message effectively.

Two Sentence Example
Example: "I would like to **TRY** to convince you that my company can serve you very well."

"I don't know if you are a viable prospect for my services. Our service is superior."
Three Sentence Example
Example: "I will **try** to get my boss to go along with this discount you have asked for."
When the prospect hears this sentence, he automatically knows you are going to fail to get this discount for him. So, he will likely turn around and ask to be given even more benefits, such as extended service at no additional charge. (This is unconscious on the customer's part, similar to a child piling demands upon a parent in hopes of getting something.)

The Correction:
1. "You have asked for an additional discount and I agree that based on the size and credit worthiness of your company, you have the right to ask that from many venders. " (In this sentence, you verify how they are thinking and acknowledge that they deserve to ask that kind of question.)
2. "It is very unlikely that our company will be able to discount this in view of our profit structure on this item.' (This sentence explains your predicament.)

3. "I will discuss it with my sales manager for you.' (This sentence lets him know that you honor your relationship and clearly indicates that you will ask the question for him.)

Using the word **TRY** is a bad habit you **DO** need to break. It is very tempting to say, "I would like to try to show you how our service will be superior for you." It is better to say, "I don't know if your needs are a match for our services. If we discover that you can use our services, I am certain I can demonstrate that our service is superior to anything else available."

The rule of thumb is: When you are tempted to say TRY you need to break the ideas into two or more sentences to give further explanation.

Delete BUT - Substitute AND

The word BUT tends to cancel out what was said before it. Consider the sentence, 'I really appreciate your giving me this appointment, but I think you will be interested in what our company has to offer.' Do you notice how the but in the middle seems to almost negate the meaning of the first part of the sentence? It almost says, "I was not sincere when I said the part about appreciating the appointment."

Whenever you are about to say the word **BUT**, simply substitute the word **AND** instead. (You probably mean and anyway as you will see.) In the above example, you would say, *'I really appreciate your giving me this appointment, and I think you will be interested in what our company has to offer.'* Besides not canceling out the first thought in a compound sentence, in many cases **AND** can also be used to add credence to the secondary thought. Do you notice how the fact that you have been given an appointment - added - *to the idea that they will be interested lends additional believability to the whole sentence?* This is usually what actually happens in the other person's mind when you use the word **AND** to connect tag-along thoughts.

The general idea here is that you can take an undeniable fact and by adding the word **AND** to some other idea, both ideas will be accepted, at least temporarily. For example, if you want to sell the idea that small companies (such as yours) have advantages over large companies (such as your competition), you could phrase it this way:

21

(UNDENIABLE FACT) "I have chosen to become a marketing representative for ZIZZ Company, **AND** (IDEA I WANT YOU TO ACCEPT) I find small companies have several advantages over larger corporations. I would like to tell you how I think these advantages can provide something useful for you and your company."

Do you notice how the first part of the sentence, because it is simply true, lends believability to the next part? Then the following idea, that the customer may gain advantage becomes a reasonable possibility. This does not mean that people will accept all of your ideas with blind faith just by using the word **AND**. It simply means they will give you the benefit of the doubt **AND** listen to your proposal before they make a judgement about its appropriateness for them.

AVOID USING OVER-GENERALIZATIONS
Avoid ALWAYS, NEVER, and ALL

All, always, and never are examples of over-generalizations. When these words are used, the listener usually begins to think of counter-examples. For instance, if you say, 'All of our customers are pleased with our service," the listener immediately searches their memory for counter- examples to your statement to discount what you JUST have said. This, too, is an automatic response that is often unconscious.

Using these words that over-generalize reduces the believability of what you say. They can also have a negative effect when trying to establish a relationship. It is usually better to offer some kind of qualification - without being wishy-washy."

Over-Generalization:
"All of our customers are pleased with our service."

More Believable:
"Our customers are very pleased with our service and have commented on how well we handle their questions and the occasional problems."

- or -

Over-Generalization:
"This dishwasher never fails."

More Believable:
"This model is very reliable and our customers rarely report problems."

After making a more believable statement, you can often go on to discuss other benefits in similar positive and realistic terms.

ADDING WORD ENDINGS MAKES A DIFFERENCE
Just as some words need to be deleted from your sales jargon, others can be changed slightly to be more effective.

There are ways to change a word to give it more impact, authority, and movement. Changing your words slightly will successfully attract more customers.

-LY Words
Words that end with -LY such as fortunately, happily, etc., have a special meaning. They give added authority and can often persuade someone to listen to you. Consider this example.

Prospect: "I do not have time to listen to you right now."

Salesman: "Excellent. You are just the kind of person we are looking for. **Fortunately**, we are available to make these kinds of calls day or night, including weekends, and I know that you would never place yourself in a position of not having **timely** information available to yourself if you had some way to get it. As I said, happily we are in a position to make this information available to you, perhaps Saturday evening."

-ING Words
A person is more likely to consider your proposal if you use words that indicate movement. Adding **-ING** to a word gives movement and action to that word.

For example:
"This machine has the capacity to copy 20 pages per minute."

- versus -

"This machine has a copying capacity of 20 pages per minute."
Many people find that the second way of saying this has more emotional impact.

"This suit makes you look like a million dollars."

- versus -

"This suit has you looking like a million dollars."

KEEP YOUR WORD TOOLS CLEAN
As you become more aware of these words, you develop the ability to determine when it is appropriate to use them. Words are your vehicle, your tool. Experience will help you to decide which tools

are appropriate when establishing and maintaining the sales relationship. Before a word leaps out of your mouth, ask yourself this question: "What do I want to accomplish?' and then choose accordingly.

SUMMARY

Periodically assess your words and behavior. Pay attention to the things you say so that they do not detract from your "sales relationship. " Notice which words and non-verbal behaviors build relationships. Make notes of what works for you and what does not. Delete those things that don't work and practice the things that do. Consciously think about specific words and actions that increase your effectiveness. By practicing these methods, you will form patterns of behavior that will become automatic.

In the next chapter, we begin to learn about the **Green Light Selling** model and you will see how important your new word skills can be.

"There's plenty of great advice available about the art of making talks, but if you don't adapt it to yourself, none of it is worth much."

-Judy Langford Carter

POINTS TO REMEMBER

1. DELETE "WHY", "TRY", AND "BUT" FROM YOUR SALES VOCABULARY
2. USE THE WORD "AND" TO TIE IMPORTANT IDEAS TOGETHER
3. WHEN TEMPTED TO SAY "TRY", USE TWO OR THREE SENTENCES INSTEAD
4. USE "-LY" AND "-ING" WORDS TO ADD IMPACT, AUTHORITY, AND MOVEMENT TO YOUR STATEMENTS

Chapter 3

YOU NEVER GET A SECOND CHANCE TO MAKE A FIRST IMPRESSION

The ENTRANCE is where you begin to build your sales relationship. Properly structured, the ENTRANCE builds the foundation for the sales relationship and pulls the transaction toward a successful OUTCOME and EXIT. Establishing relationships is like buying insurance. Like insurance, relationships, from time to time, need to be renewed.

Every sales situation (or communication) has a minimum of two things. An Entrance and an Exit. The end result of any selling interaction depends heavily on the quality of your Entrance. From the beginning, it is essential that your mind remains focused toward your end point or Exit. What is your goal? What are you determined to accomplish by the end of this sales call? Remembering the Amateur and Professional, if you don't have a procedure for getting from Entrance to Exit ... you'll wind up lost.

> "There's no room for amateurs, even in crossing the streets."
> George Segal

In the very first moments of our interactions, we influence others by the way we use our voice, body, and words. Ninety-three percent of the impression you make is determined by how you look and sound. By learning specific language patterns and becoming aware of what your prospects are seeing and hearing, you begin to have more fun and become more artful in your Entrance skills.

You enter each sales situation with much to offer - information, willingness to serve, the resources of your product, and the company that stands behind you. Now, with the **Green Light Selling** model, you can really use your experience and promote your company with excellence. Successfully completing the Entrance by using the ideas below move you toward that goal.

ALWAYS KEEP RELATIONSHIP FIRST

Two prospective companies (Eagle Janitorial and Kleen-UP) are selling similar products to SR Industries. Even the proposals these two companies have submitted are similar. What is the determining factor that the buyer at SR Industries will use to select their supplier? HE WILL GIVE HIS MONEY TO THE SALESPERSON WITH WHOM HE FEELS THE GREATEST RELATIONSHIP.

People want to be treated as if a "relationship' with them is the most important reason for your sales interaction. We all want to feel valuable for ourselves, not just our pocket- book.

> If relationship is not established at the Entrance, it is unlikely that it will ever exist.

You can lose the sale by failing to demonstrate that your first priority is to form a continuing bond. Establishing a relationship not only promotes the possibility of your first sale, it begins the possibility of continuing referrals. Everything you do has to key off of this central "relationship first" idea. At no time can you violate it. If at any time you do violate the relationship, you won't get the sale. The keynote to all sales is RELATIONSHIP, RELATIONSHIP, RELATIONSHIP.

Test This Idea Out For Yourself
> a. At some time, you have needed to select someone that you wanted on your side - be it a lawyer, accountant, or insurance agent. Now go back and think about your very first interaction with the individual YOU SELECTED. In all probability, money was not the major consideration. You will find that what originally impressed you was their insistence upon relationship **first**.
> b. Maybe you have recently purchased an item that could have been bought from two or more different people. In all probability, you bought from the person who communicated "relationship" to you, even if the cost was a little higher.

VERBAL AND NON-VERBAL COMMUNICATION
When you meet with a prospect, you generally engage in what is commonly referred to as small talk. We are always communicating by giving both verbal and non-verbal messages. On the surface, you may appear to be discussing the weather or the local basketball team. On a non-verbal level however, you are both sizing one another up (establishing relationship) before getting into the real reason for your meeting. During this time, it is especially critical that you, as a salesperson, keep your conversation free of any hint of bias or

judgement. If you offend a prospect's belief system, the sale is dead. That is it. Again, "relationship first" is the outcome you want to achieve.

You are always communicating something.
Voice tones, facial expressions, slight changes in your body posture, even the way you dress are all forms of communication. These non-verbal signals of communication are constantly being read and interpreted by others. In the first few moments (roughly the first 12 seconds) of any interaction, these signals are quickly flashing between you and your customer. You might have heard them called "vibes." Non-verbal signals allow you and the other person to learn a great deal about each other in a short period of time.

> "I present myself to you in a form suitable to the relationship I wish to achieve with you."
> -Luigi Pirandello

Some ways to non-verbally communicate relationship are: a friendly smile, a relaxed posture, holding someone's hand a few moments longer than is necessary when you shake it, and assuming a posture that is similar to your client's posture. These examples of non-verbal communication say, "I am like you." They build rapport and move your mutual boundaries closer. When you offer these non-verbal signals, people have a tendency to extend courtesies to you as if you had already established a relationship.

Many years ago, I purchased a Rolex watch because I wanted a visible, external sign that time was important to me - my time and the customer's time. I found that Rolex wearers have a tendency to notice other Rolex wearers and never mention it. When a Rolex wearer sees a Rolex wearer or a BMW driver sees another BMW driver, it's like belonging to the same club. As near as I can recall, in the many years that I have been selling, I have never failed to sell to a prospect who also wore a Rolex. It was automatically presupposed by the client that as a Rolex wearer, I had values that were similar to theirs. Somehow I was "like them." By wearing this watch, I was in an instantaneous relationship.

Matching Their Personality
Certain status symbols are appropriate. Each business organization has its own culture or style that it is comfortable with. At a

minimum, there will be a dress code and a range of acceptable behaviors (which probably exists as an unspoken organizational agreement). You should match yourself to the client's organizational style as much as you can. If you show up on your sales call dressed in a rock-and-roll T-shirt and Bermuda shorts, you will NOT sell well to the 3-piece suit crowd. They won't even hear you. Of course, a 3-piece suit won't sell well to the T-shirt crowd either.

Ask yourself, "Do I look and act like I could fit in as one of them?"

By not wearing an appropriate suit in a business setting, you could risk failure. Put on the uniform that is appropriate for your product. The uniform communicates to your customer that you are the same, because you are both willing to wear the uniform. You may be offering all the right words to your prospect, but if your non-verbal signals aren't congruent with your words, you reach a RED LIGHT.

INITIAL BENEFIT STATEMENT
The very first communication you have with your prospect is the Initial Benefit Statement. This is a statement of why you are there and it should focus on your prospect; exuding the relationship you are creating in the same way the smell of fresh baked bread causes you to think of home-cooked food. This statement gives your purpose or what can be accomplished with your product or service (Outcome). It is issued sometime during those first critical moments of interaction between you and your prospectus). While it is not essential that your prospects completely believe your words, it is crucial that your communication generates enough interest so they will listen to you, at least for a few moments.

The Formula
For your opening, I recommend a three-step process.
1. Identification - Identify who you are.
2. Purpose - A general statement of why you are there.
3. Give them an option - Ask "Do you want me to tell you about my proposal, or would you prefer that I show you the printed material first?" Something along those lines, to ask them if they would like to HEAR first or SEE first.

Your opening statement should be delivered in a way that indicates that relationship is a priority. When you get to giving them an option, follow their lead. Depending on their response, you either tell them about your product first or show them first. Your closing question is then, "How do you feel about it?" Here is an example of a typical Initial Benefit Statement that you could give if you were selling air purification equipment:

Example
"I'm from Ace Air Purification Systems. I hope to be able to assist you in reducing the radon hazard of the air in your home. I don't know if I can do that or not, but I know how to find out. Would it be possible for me to talk with you for a few minutes or show you my presentation?"

"I Don't Know if.... "
Your Initial Benefit Statement identifies your particular product and what you believe it will accomplish for your prospect. No matter what you are selling, the statement, "I don't know if I can be of any assistance to you in this regard or not, but I know how to find out. " could probably be included. This statement verbalizes what the prospect is thinking while you are talking. They do not know if you can be of assistance or not; part of them may suspect you can and another part suspects you cannot. Adding this statement puts your prospect more at ease by indirectly addressing their thoughts. Your prospects are more likely to listen to you if your attitude verbally and non-verbally communicates "relationship."

Power Words
Use as many words as possible from the "Power Word List" when you are constructing your Initial Benefit Statement. These words add impact and interest to supercharge your opening statement.

Power Word List

• ADVANTAGES	• CUTTING EDGE
• CONFIDENT	• SOLID
• CHALLENGE	• CONSISTENT
• DEMONSTRATE	• USEFUL
• DESIGN	• EXPECT
• CONVENIENCE	• EFFECTIVE
• HIGH-TECH	• LOGICAL

The following example gives you an idea of how to weave these words into your Initial Benefit Statement:

Example

"One of the main ADVANTAGES you can EXPECT from the product is the CONVENIENCE it will provide. Many HIGH-TECH companies have accepted the CHALLENGE of being on the CUTTING EDGE by using this UNIQUE approach. SOLID engineering and EFFECTIVE planning have gone into the DESIGN of this product, which gives it a SPECIAL STYLE. I am here today to DEMONSTRATE how this product can SECURE additional profits for you."

OUTCOME

While formulating your Initial Benefit Statement, always keep the finish line in mind. It is important in your introduction to let the client know you are there for them. It is also important to know what you want to accomplish in your communication BEFORE you start. Even if you are setting up a future appointment, you must decide before your ENTRANCE what you want to accomplish before you EXIT.

"A thought which does not result in action is nothing much, and an action which does not proceed from a thought is nothing at all. "
-Georges Bernanos

It has been said that it is easier to pull a string than to push one. A specific outcome/objective formulated at the Entrance will help pull you through the sales process by focusing your attention, energizing you, and directing your effort. You have reached a well-formed outcome (goal) when both salesperson and client have a joint target or agenda that they agree upon. This joint outcome must also be stated in sensory specific terms. That is, it must be expressed in a tangible form (something you can see, hear, touch, etc.) that is real to both of you.

A well-formed outcome or objective might be:

Example

"I would like to show you how this XYZ product will speed up your operation...."

Without an outcome in mind, how will either the salesman or the client know when they are finished? With a clearly defined outcome, the salesman and the client will have essentially the same picture in their minds to work toward - a common goal. This joint objective/goal transaction must also take place within the first minutes of your encounter, either right after the Initial Benefit Statement or within it.

Example
"I'm from XYZ Systems. I hope to make your manufacturing more efficient. I don't know if I can do that or not, but I know how to find out. Would it be possible for me to talk to you for a few minutes? I would like to show you how this XYZ product will speed up your operations."

Without a direction or target to shoot for, the conversation with your prospect has a tendency to be meaningless and wander. Most sales situations do wander and are extremely inefficient. Tom Peters, author of Thriving on Chaos, makes it very clear that a meeting for information only is a meeting of no value. A sales process that begins with no verbal indication of an end objective by salesman or prospect is of no value.

"If you are resolutely determined to make something of yourself, the thing is more than half done already. Always bear in mind that your own resolution to succeed is more important than any other one thing."
-Abraham Lincoln

FIRST QUESTION OR STATEMENT IN ESTABLISHING RELATIONSHIPS

After the Initial Benefit Statement, you need a vehicle to develop a relationship with your clients. The "ice breakers" below are examples of opening statements we have all tried. Which ones do you think would be most effective to start a productive RELATIONSHIP at your Entrance?

Possible Starter Questions
"What areas of your business would you like increased?"

"How do you happen to be here?"

"How much do you earn for this type of work?"

"If you had more money to spend, how would you spend it?"

"What do you like to do in your spare time?"

"Do you have a family?"

"Do you live in the city or in a suburb?"

"How do you feel about ... ?"

"Do you or anyone in your family have ... ?"

"I was referred to you by - - .'

"You probably have been thinking about..."
Words are the tools you consciously use everyday to communicate. Your words can form a lasting relationship or not, depending on the language patterns you use. When you first meet someone, there are only a few different types of topics that make sense to talk about. The questions you ask in your first interaction can usually be classified in one of six categories.

PERSONAL: "Do you have a family?" "I was refined to you by - - - " "How do you happen to be here?" " Do you know so and so?"
(Questions about the person and their family.)

AVOCATION: "What do you like to do in your spare time?"
(Questions about their hobbies or special interests.)

LOCATION: "Do you live in the city or in a suburb?"
(Questions about where they live and where they are from.)

VOCATION: "What areas of your business would you like increased?"
(Questions about the kind of work they do.)

INFORMATION: "If you had more money to spend, how would you spend it?"
(Questions about what they want to know or learn.)

MONEY: "How much do you earn?"
(Questions about your source and amount of income. Be aware, many people find this type of question offensive.)

Of these six content categories above, the best ones to help you establish "relationship first" are questions from the Personal and

Avocation categories. My first question when meeting someone used to be "What kind of work do you do?" My question was intended to search out facts and meeting places in an effort to discover how we might have something to talk about. The question I now ask is "How do you happen to be here in the first place?" because it is a "relationship first" question. What were your choices from the list of possible starter questions?

You can also establish relationship very quickly by asking about family. In most conversations, it is easy to relate most subjects in that direction. For example, you could be talking about the weather and say, "Looks like we are going to have a wonderful weekend. Do you typically go out with your family on the weekend and do things or is that work time for you?" Most people respond positively to this show of interest. However, be very aware of the response you receive. In this age of rapidly changing relationships, family can also be a "touchy area." Always keep finely tuned into your client and be flexible if their responses indicate you need to change direction rapidly.

> "You can't be all things to all people. But I can be all things to the people I select.
> -Donald Neuensch Wander

Finding a common avocation can gain amazing camaraderie. If you can find a common avocation that is somewhat unusual (such as if both of you happen to be 5-string banjo players), that is terrific. By asking relationship questions, you can move toward locating an avocation that you can explore. Discovering a common avocation at the Entrance often establishes a relationship with your prospect that can move you easily through the **Green Light Selling** model to your planned Exit.

For example, a man who wanted a life insurance policy had been approached by three different companies without success. It happened that this man was an avid golfer. When introduced to a representative who was also an avid golfer (and who had played some of the same courses), the resulting sale of a half-million dollar policy was accomplished quickly.

BALANCE YOUR GIVE WITH TAKE
I have noticed that if one person is doing all of the giving in a

relationship, the other person will learn that they don't have to give. This also happens in the sales relationship. You must create the balance of "give and take" at the ENTRANCE. At some point, your prospect needs to give. However, the client will NOT GIVE if you have trained them otherwise by demonstrating all the giving yourself. The prospect will not want to reciprocate. They will be so conditioned to receiving that the process of shifting gears to become a giver may take longer than you are willing to wait.

> "Once the toothpaste is out of the tube, its hard to get it back in."
> -H.R. Haldeman

These unbalanced relationships fall apart because the customer is not responding to you quickly enough. Wayne Dyer in his book, Your Erroneous Zones, said, "You've got to teach them how to treat you right away.' John Grinder, co-developer with Richard Bandler of Neuro-Linguistic Programming (NLP), called it "symmetry" in the relationship. In couples therapy sessions, Grinder would ask one person to make a change and then ask the other person to make a change. By having both participants make a change, it maintained the symmetry in the relationship. No one gave more than the other. In the business world, contracts require that same idea of symmetry in the relationship. If you don't start with symmetry in the selling setting, you may never get to it. Establish it in the **ENTRANCE.**

REFERRALS: BUILT-IN RELATIONSHIP
Referrals are wonderful. They are an oasis in opening sales relationships. For a brief period of time, you are offered what appears to be an established relationship. Consider this situation. You know Peter and your new prospect also knows Peter. So when you introduce yourself with your Initial Benefit Statement, you can say to your prospect, "Peter and I have been working together and he suggested I talk to you because you might also enjoy this (product, or service).' Because your prospect already has a relationship with Peter, he will instantaneously and unconsciously offer you the same degree of trust and information that he would give to Peter, at least for a few minutes. That is why referrals are such a valuable resource.

> **Knowing a person in common can be used in a similar fashion to a referral when establishing a new sales relationship.**

STAY AWARE AND FLEXIBLE

Flexibility
It is said that the most flexible part of any system is the strongest and eventually controls the outcome. This is also true in the sales situation. If you (the salesperson) remain the most flexible in your interaction (especially with a rigid and domineering prospect), you will be in control of the outcome. This element of flexibility is very important when using the **Green Light Selling** model.

Your prospects are going to spend their money with someone. So, it might as well be with you, right? However, if you do not establish a relationship, even though you probably have an excellent service or product that the customer needs, you won't get the order. This is how it works. Because you offer what the customer needs, it will be hard for them to say no, but without "relationship" they won't say yes either. As a result, you will spend a lot of time between your Entrance and your Exit and probably Exit without the order. Time is expensive. If you have not established relationship at the beginning or have somehow violated it beyond the point of reclamation, it is usually better to take your losses and leave quickly. Learn from your mistakes and then roll down the road and do better next time.

There are exceptions to this rule. This is where flexibility in your behavior can make a difference. If you are aware that you have not established a firm relationship, you can sometimes salvage the situation. This takes polish, conviction, and (as in many last ditch efforts) some "dumb luck. "

The Last Ditch Save Formula
First, you close out the old relationship by CREATING an Exit (this finishes out the old communication). Then you re-enter (a new Entrance) with an attitude that says, "You know that guy you used to deal with? He just turned over a new leaf. This is the new him standing before you." In order for this to work effectively, your words and non-verbal signals must match (you must look like you mean it). By changing one or more of your non-verbal elements (a shift in your posture or a voice tone shift), the prospect will know that somehow you HAVE changed. When you indicate this change you have to be congruent; believing inside what you are showing

and saying on the outside. If you can't redeem the relationship, save everyone's time and move on down the road.

"Try, try, try again. And then quit. There is no sense in making a damn fool of yourself."
-W. C. Fields

POINTS TO REMEMBER-
1. KEEP RELATIONSHIP FIRST
2. BECOME MORE AWARE OF YOUR VERBAL AND NON-VERBAL MESSAGES
3. CREATE AND PRACTICE YOUR INITIAL BENEFIT STATEMENT
4. ALWAYS KEEP YOUR OUTCOME IN MIND
5. ASK PERSONAL AND AVOCATIONAL QUESTIONS
6. USE REFERRALS TO ESTABLISH RELATIONSHIP WHEN POSSIBLE
7. STRIVE TO MAINTAIN SYMMETRY IN YOUR RELATIONSHIPS
8. BE AWARE OF THE SITUATION AT HAND AND REMAIN FLEXIBLE

Chapter 4

RAPPORT: THE MAGIC OF RELATIONSHIP

If you put many business meetings under a microscope, amazing dynamics are exposed. Individuals are vying for positions, department heads are busy protecting their budgets, and there is a general lack of cooperation because people feel threatened. Unless it is established before a meeting that the topics discussed will not harm the current position of the participants, the meeting will go nowhere. Few action items can or will be accomplished because the participants will not want to contribute. They will not be committed to the process.

> **"Many attempts to communicate are nullified by saying too much.**
> -Robeil Greenleaf

In much the same way, salespeople are often called upon to make their presentations to customers who are also protective of their positions and feel threatened. This can give "cold call" a whole new meaning - selling to "ice people" is not fun. However, if the tone of the sales encounter is set up so that the customer does not feel threatened or afraid of expressing their ideas, a successful interaction can take place. The magical component that can make a meeting happen is rapport.

John Grinder, said it best, "Rapport is responsiveness." When people are in a state of rapport, they are more likely to respond positively to one another. Rapport can put the life back into "ice people.' Learning specific techniques that help create rapport with your customers increases your sales effectiveness.

Interactions between people are primarily learning experiences. We learn from one another by solving problems together and discovering new points of view. There wouldn't be much rationale for getting together if both parties could not benefit from the interaction.

- **In a sense, selling is a learning experience a coming together to assist and discover.**

In order for a selling scenario to be conducive to learning, the customer we approach has to believe that he is safe enough to participate. If the customer perceives that the situation doesn't feel safe enough, no exchange of quality information will transpire and the meeting will be of little value (to anyone except perhaps to your competitors).

The **Green Light Selling** model is structured to help you achieve and maintain rapport with your customer throughout the sales process. Your ENTRANCE sets the stage, creating an environment where both seller and prospect can feel comfortable. Your Initial Benefit Statement can also address this issue. The well-formed OUTCOME (objective) you and your client agree upon (in sensory specific terms) during your first few minutes allows you to learn what the client is comfortable talking about.

You can work together toward a common outcome by creating a common goal and sense of direction. Your purpose now is to define the limitations that your prospect wants to work within. If you discover that the prospect is not comfortable with certain areas, you can narrow the agenda until they can participate fully. As soon as you can come down to a well-formed outcome (that they feel safe to move toward), then you and your client can respond fully to each other within that specific context (frame).

The Importance of Rapport
I recently walked into a video store to pass the time while my wife was running some errands. I walked over to look at a video camera. A young man came over to me in an excited and overly helpful manner immediately asking, "So, you are looking to get yourself a video camera?" I said no. Everything about the way he had approached me was wrong. There is no way after he inappropriately approached me that he could have sold me anything from that point on. The salesman didn't come over and attempt to create some general rapport with me. He didn't meet me as a person - he only saw me as a potential sale. From then on, there was nothing he could do to make me want to know him. Frankly, I couldn't get out of the store fast enough.

The idea of creating rapport to allow a sales situation to manifest was first explicated by John Grinder. He first systemized the different levels of rapport. The **Green Light Selling** model has changed the terminology so that it may apply more directly to business. The essential ideas are still the same and equally important.

FRAMING THE THREE LEVELS OF RAPPORT

There are three levels of rapport that need to be accomplished before you can move on through the **Green Light Selling** process. Think of each level of rapport as a frame or context within which some activity is happening. The frame is where the borders of perception exist.

The largest outside frame of rapport (Level 1) is called the Safety Zone (SZ); next smaller frame of rapport (Level 2) is called Personal Responsiveness (PR); enclosed within Level 1 and 2 is the next frame of rapport (Level 3) called Leveraged Outcome (LO). When all three levels of rapport are intact, then the salesperson is then able to use their other sales tools successfully.

Picture each level of rapport as an enclosure or a box. Each box is nested within the other; smaller boxes are enclosed in larger boxes. Or, think of an excursion to the store. Level 1: You must enter the door to get inside. Level 2: You must travel inside the store to find what you want to purchase. Level 3: You must locate a salesperson. Only after you locate the salesperson can you purchase your item.

Level I - Safety Zone (SZ)

Before people can engage in and benefit from an interaction with other people, they must have a feeling of safety. This feeling of safety establishes the sides of the outside box. The Safely Zone is the first level of rapport.

Each person's criteria for feeling safe depends partly on where they live. If an individual was raised in a small town in Idaho, they will view the world differently than people raised in New York City. What about your customer? Is the world they live in a dangerous or friendly place? People learn the answer to this question early in childhood and conduct themselves accordingly. People become astute at observing how others around them behave in different contexts and have the tendency to pattern their behavior after those around them. People come to expect their world to operate a particular way. Everything that operates within their expectations is considered safe. You have to respect this safety zone. If the customer's expectations are violated by inappropriate or unexpected behavior, they will be startled into a state of alertness. Any approach by someone with an unknown intent can mobilize this state of alertness or wariness into action.

What You Can Do
A friendly attitude and intention of offering help and service does much to reassure your prospect. Using the principle of relationship you learned in the previous chapter will help you establish the first level of rapport by building a Safety Zone (SZ). You have evidence in your own experience of what this feels like. Between friends, it means feeling safe enough to confide your deepest secrets. In a class, it means feeling relaxed enough to pay attention to the instructor. In a business situation, it means developing enough trust to listen to the salesperson and eventually exchanging money for a product or service.

Level 2 - Personal Responsiveness (PR)
Once the safety zone is established, a person will allow Personal Responsiveness (PR) to develop.

The conditions required for this second level of rapport are met when the individuals are responding to each other rather than paying attention to traffic outside or a conversation in the next room. When two people are at this level of rapport, they are genuinely interested in each other. They also begin matching each other's verbal and non-verbal behaviors (pacing). The salesperson might say, "I would like to show you our new line of products. Do you have a few minutes right now?" Agreement by the prospect is evidence of Level 2 Rapport.

Rapport Through Pacing
Non-verbal rapport can be gained by pacing. Pacing is when you are verbally and non-verbally matching another's behavior. You have probably watched close friends or acquaintances unconsciously leaning forward toward each other as they talk. This is Level 2 Rapport in action. This matching makes the one you are communicating with feel more comfortable because you are indicating that you are "alike" in some way. In the sales context, the salesperson can approximate the prospect's voice tone and tempo or body posture and movements until they are responding to each other naturally. To an outsider watching this level of rapport, both salesman and customer would appear comfortable and responsive to

one another.

Be very respectful in your pacing. You are not your client's mirror and a 'monkey see monkey do' approach will, in most cases, lose the sale immediately and forever. Do not mimic.

Pacing means that you temporarily place your agenda on hold, and commit your attention and effort to the task of assuming the other person's perceptual position. This does not mean that you necessarily agree with their way of thinking, it only means that you do what you can to indicate a willingness to appreciate their point of view. Pacing in the business context is best thought of as active listening. Pay attention to what the person says and how they say it. So if you feel compelled to say or do something ... say and do it so that they will be comfortable with HOW you present your information.

An Example of Curing a Mismatch By Pacing
A Trainer for a large company was trying to get the managers to bring their people into seminars. He kept sending lengthy memos to the Head Manager to no avail. After comparing the two styles of memos, it was obvious that there was a total mismatch. The Head Manager always wrote 4 paragraphs on one 8 1/2 " by 11 " piece of paper and each paragraph had 2 to 4 sentences. The Trainer's memo was 2 to 3 pages long, single spaced, and contained only 3 paragraphs in the entire document. It was obvious that the Head Manager never read the memos because they totally mismatched his personal style. I advised the Trainer to send a memo in the Head Manager's style. The Trainer changed the format, and he was finally understood by the Head Manager.

Talk Little ... Listen Much
Most salespeople talk too much and need to listen more. The talker is the buyer. The salesperson needs to pace more so the buyer will talk. Other ways to pace in a business sense are clothing, grooming, tone of voice, and educational level of language. Maintain your awareness at all times. What is going on with them? You may be wondering how you will be able to remember to do all of this while you are trying to conduct a reasonable sales call. There is a simple solution. The procedure is to develop the habit of pacing.

Pacing Posture and Voice Tones

Next time you are with others, notice how you relate to them. Most likely you are already unconsciously pacing people around you. Pacing is something most people do naturally. Top sales performers invariably pace the postures and voice tones of their prospects with great skill. You might guess that this is a natural consequence of taking a sincere interest in the outcomes of your customers, and you would probably be right.

Pacing postures is simply making sure that your body is in more or less the same general configuration as your prospect. If the prospect is sitting erect with their hands clasped in front of them, you do the same. If they cross their legs, you cross yours. If they look at your literature, you look at it too. Remember, you are not a robot or a monkey. If you can't be natural and unobtrusive, don't pace the client.

Pacing voice tones is the process of making sure that you sound more or less the same way they sound. If they speak quickly, you speak a bit more quickly. If they have a high voice, raise the pitch of your voice a little. You are not trying to sound exactly like them, but do make sure that you do not sound radically different.

The most important caution we can offer you at this point is: don't get caught. Many people have had specific training in these pacing techniques. We have seen people pace so badly that it was insulting. Others have learned proper pacing skills, which have significantly increased their sales. These are the people who were able to gracefully pace postures and voice tones without being obvious. Practice pacing postures and voice tones. It is a way of staying "in touch" with your prospect, not a way to manipulate them. Having the right attitude about pacing provides another benefit: you will automatically notice if they momentarily get out of rapport with you.

Level 3 - Leveraged Outcome (LO)

Leveraged Outcome (LO) is established when you and your prospect have reached agreement about what they want to accomplish. The outcome is their stated objective. The leverage comes by getting a firm agreement about what your prospect wants. Here is an example of a typical outcome being leveraged.

> Salesperson: "So you are fairly sure that $150,000 in insurance would meet the needs of your family in the event you became disabled?"

Prospect: "Sure. I guess that sounds about right.

Salesperson: (Notes lack of conviction.) "Do I understand, from what you are saying, that you are committed to making sure that some arrangements are made for your family in case something happens to you, but you are still uncertain about the exact amount?"

Prospect: "No. I'm pretty sure the amount is right, but I have some doubt about making a commitment at this time."

Salesperson: (Leveraging the amount.) "So you are absolutely determined to provide $150,000 in coverage for your family."

Prospect: 'That's right."

At this point, the salesperson has leveraged (gained an affirmative commitment) the amount of insurance his client wants. From this point forward in the sales situation, the prospect will have difficulty waffling on this part of the issue. Next, the salesperson would do a similar maneuver relative to the timing of the commitment (to obtain the full leveraged outcome).

To establish and maintain the leverage, it is important to state your prospect's outcome in words that they agree with and then you must remember those words. If they should later lose track of their objective, you can gently remind them of what they first said they wanted, in their own words. Your job, as a master communicator and the leader in your selling conversation, is to make sure you are *working toward your customer's leveraged outcome at all times.*

Now You Can Use Your Tools

- **With the leveraged outcome frame intact, you are free to make use of your tools.**

Tools

Your tools include your knowledge about people, information about your product or service, the methods of selling you have developed, and your personal style. You bring into the selling situation all of the abilities and talents you have which are appropriate for this context. Among these are the social skills you possess that allow you to communicate with other people.

RECOVERING WHEN RAPPORT SLIPS

Most skilled salespersons CAN intuitively start the sales call with finesse. They usually do something to insure that the prospect is reasonably comfortable with the overall situation (Establishing Safety Zone -SZ). Then they do something to get the prospect to respond to them and their presentation (Establishing Personal Responsiveness - PR). Then they begin to relate to the prospect's needs (Establishing their Leveraged Outcome - LO).

It is usually when they get to Level 3 (Leveraged Outcome) that even seasoned salespersons begin to make serious errors. They do not spend adequate time getting the outcome leveraged. This can lead to problems later. Therefore, we suggest that you take those extra few moments required to get **solid** Leveraged Outcomes.

> **"Problems are only opportunities in work clothes."**
> -Henry J. Kaiser

Most sales people are fairly clever at getting into their tools. They begin to tell a little about their company, their product, and do what they can to gather useful information from the prospect. Problems seem to crop up just when the prospect is beginning to show real interest.

We have noticed that as the prospect "warms up," the salesperson often begins to get more and more involved in his/her tools. This means the salesperson may be paying more attention to their "pitch" than to the responses of their prospect. If they proceed in this manner, the salesperson might as well write it all down and mail it to the dead letter office because the customer is not listening. The prospect has dropped out of rapport. Most professionals have had this experience at least once. Fortunately, the situation is redeemable.

The Fastest and Best Way to Recover Rapport is to:
1. **Pause.** Don't even attempt to come to a graceful stopping place. Once you realize that your prospect has "gone away," you might as well just stop.

2. **Check Safety Zone (SZ)** This is simply a quick check to make sure you have not gone beyond the limits of the relationship. You must confine your discussions to those

subjects that are clearly appropriate to the relationship at this time. For example, it is seldom possible to interject political or religious biases without violating the Safety Zone (SZ). If you have inadvertently done something like that, you need to quickly extricate yourself from the mess you have created.

3. **Check Personal Responsiveness (PR)** Everyone is responding to something all the time. Make sure they are still responding to you. If they are not, do whatever is necessary to bring them back.

4. **Check Leveraged Outcome (LO)** You may have done or said something that got the prospect off track. If you are talking about one outcome and they are thinking about another outcome, you need to get things back on track.

5. **Return to your Tools** If the Safety Zone (SZ), Personal Responsiveness (PR), and Leveraged Outcome (LO) frames are all intact, it is safe to resume selling. If any of these frames are not intact, you are probably wasting your time. Continue to monitor the integrity of these frames as you use your selling tools.

If you are pacing your prospects with respect, in order to make them comfortable, you will naturally stop (Step 1, above) *if any of the rapport frames is lost. Then, you can simply do the next Steps (2, 3, 4, and 5) and continue with your work.*

Now that you have your customer in a state of receptiveness, you are ready to slide into the next step in the sales process. You will begin to really understand how our top sales performers make selling look so fun and easy.

POINTS TO REMEMBER-
1. ESTABLISH / MAINTAIN SAFETY ZONE(SZ), PERSONAL RESPONSIVENESS (PR), AND LEVERAGED OUTCOME (LO)
2. PACE POSTURE AND VOICE TONES
3. DON'T PACE TOO OBVIOUSLY

4. MAKE PERIODIC CHECKS TO MAKE SURE YOU ARE STILL MAINTAINING ALL THREE RAPPORT FRAMES
5. RECOVER RAPPORT IF ANY OF THE THREE RAPPORT FRAMES ARE LOST

Chapter 5

MAKING SURE THERE ARE GREEN LIGHTS ALL THE WAY

For a moment, think of the selling process as similar to traveling down a street with stop lights at each intersection. How would you respond if at each intersection you encountered a red light? What if you had to stop at each red light AND get out of your car AND figure out how to change the light to green? Compare that to driving down the same street when each potential light is green instead. Eliciting your prospect's procedure is finding out ahead of time what it takes to turn each light green before you reach it; insuring that you will have "green lights all the way."

Establishing the three levels of rapport allows you to move easily into this next phase of the Green Light Selling model. Setting green lights is accomplished during the information gathering phase. In this step, you can HELP your prospect to make a decision (to buy your product, to shift suppliers, or to purchase more) and cause some activity on their part. By discovering your prospect's buying strategy (how they buy), they WILL HELP YOU make the sale. Because it is necessary for you to use the techniques of Backtracking and Conditional Close to smoothly elicit your prospect's buying strategy, we cover these two techniques first by learning about LOGICAL LEVELS.

SHIFTING LOGICAL LEVELS

There are two types of requirements in the world. There are Single Option Requirements and there are Multiple Option Requirements. Essentially your customer's buying reality falls somewhere between Single Option and Multiple Option Requirements. With the Single Option, the need/specification is so rigidly defined that only one solution (product, event, etc.) can possibly fulfill the requirement. Essentially, there is only ONE solution to the problem. For example, the Hope Diamond is a Single Option Requirement commodity. There is no substitute for it. Either you have the original or you don't.

In the other case, Multiple Option Requirements, the need/specification is broad enough to accommodate several possible solutions. An example of this is a customer who wants a fast, red sports car. There are many fast, red sports cars from which to choose that-could fill the customer's order. The requirement is more general and therefore leaves more options open as possible solutions.

Naturally, the Single Option customer can be more difficult to help than one who is more open to possible solutions (Multiple Options). If the Single Option customer only wants a Green, Left-Handed Widget imported from Tibet, they aren't going to buy a Red, Right-Handed Mini-Widget from Detroit. Your job is to help them shift logical levels or broaden the perceived value of what they want, moving from unique to more general.

> **"Sometimes you just have to look reality in the eye and deny it."**
> **-Garrison Keillor**

In the business context, someone may say, "I need a computer with the following characteristics (Single Option). " Unfortunately, there may be only one computer that has those specific characteristics. It is also possible that no computer could fulfill those characteristics. As a salesperson, you need to know what is behind their list of requirements; what objective does the client want to accomplish?

Your job is to help the customer find several ways to meet their objective beyond their "hard and fast' list of requirements. When the customer expands their perception and realizes that "they don't absolutely need" their particular list of requirements, they have shifted logical levels.

When people have a need, they have a tendency to decide there is only one "specific way" for them to accomplish their requirement. They become blind to any other possible alternatives that may also meet their needs.

I know someone who went from Arizona to Pensacola, Florida to get a particular Cadillac. The same individual also went to Switzerland to get a particular airplane. It is very, very seldom anyone actually NEEDS that one particular item, although they may believe that they do. If you don't happen to have a particular 1964 Mustang, does that mean you can't satisfy their need? The answer is NO! It means that you need to find a way to get beyond their current limited view and discover their real need.

"The foolish and the dead alone never change their opinion."
-James Russell Lowell

You have to help them shift logical levels and find out what they want to accomplish. "You need this so you can do what?" You can almost always offer something. What you offer could even be better for the customer than what they currently think they need. You help them expand their opinion about their available options by shifting logical levels.

Examples of Shifting Logical Levels

Example:	So You Can Do What?	What I Can Supply To Customer Instead
1964 MUSTANG	Own a collector's item	1965 Collector's Edition Mustang with Original Red Paint
A blue Floral Bedspread	Match my wallpaper	A solid stripe bedspread that matches wallpaper
A gold ring with a diamond	Be perceived as successful	A platinum ring with diamonds
An Ansel Adams print	Own a nature picture	A large selection of nature photos and prints by various artists
Industrial wall to wall carpet	Nice kitchen carpet that will wear well	Carpet designed specifically for kitchen use

There are two processes used to help your customer shift logical levels. They are: 1. Backtrack, and 2. Conditional Close.

BACKTRACK

For communications to be meaningful, you must be satisfied that other people hear you. For your prospects to feel they have communicated with you, it is necessary for you to acknowledge what they say and give any appropriate feedback. Backtracking, used throughout the selling process, tells other people, "I hear you. I

50

acknowledge that you have needs. I want to understand what you mean."

- **You use the backtrack when someone has made a statement, asked a question, or offered some kind of objection.**

To backtrack, you repeat back or paraphrase to the person what was just said, usually beginning with a brief preface, such as, "So, if I understand correctly..." or "I see, so you... " or "Let me see if I understand you fully... " Most backtracks start with the word SO. The word SO is a shorthand label that says, "I am about to comment on what you just said." A backtrack needs to begin with the word SO or a word like it to let them know -you're referring to what they just said.

Sometimes it is beneficial to begin a backtrack by stating a simple "Yes" said with an exhale of your breath and your voice tone dropping at the end. However, saying Yes while inhaling and raising of your voice tone will be misinterpreted. A yes said with an inhale says, "Yes, but - I am not really listening to you." A yes said with an exhale says, "I hear you.' Experiment for yourself. Say, "Yes" with an inhale and an exhale. Notice the difference.

Voicing A Question Or Statement
This lowering or raising of voice tone at the end of a sentence also indicates whether the words being said are meant as a question or a statement. It is imperative to your rapport that your prospects have the feeling that you are listening to them. It is equally imperative that they understand whether you are making a statement or asking a question. A statement sounds like a statement when your voice tone lowers at the end. When you are asking a question, clearly indicate that is the case by raising your voice tone when you finish the sentence. It is easier for your prospects to respond to your backtracks when you pay attention to your voice inflection. This helps the customer determine if you are asking a question or making a statement.

PROSPECT: "We must have delivery by Thursday."

BACKTRACK: "Does that mean you have a special requirement for making sure that it arrives by Thursday?" (Voice raises at end of question.)

PROSPECT: "The training process that you are proposing is way beyond the requirements of this organization."

BACKTRACK: "So, if I understand correctly, you want to make sure that the training you do fills the requirement of your current sales force." (Voice lowers at end of statement.)

PROSPECT: What I really want is a car that gets 45 miles to the gallon and is big enough for all six kids to fit in without crowding."

BACKTRACK: "Let me see if I understand fully. You want a car that is both economical and big enough to hold your family without crowding. " (Voice lowers at end of statement.)

Half-Second Rule

If your backtrack matches your prospect's experience, (their perception or understanding of what is going on), they will let you know non-verbally and verbally. The first answer they give will be non-verbal, following the half-second rule. This rule states that when people understand your question or have figured out the idea you are presenting, they answer you non-verbally within a half-second. This non-verbal response is automatic. You can detect their non-verbal answer in various facial expressions, head movements, and body movements. Usually, people move their heads up and down for, "Yes", shake them back and forth for,"No", and shrug their shoulders or some other part of their body for, "I don't know", to indicate their answer.

The verbal response follows a second or two later and may confirm or contradict the non-verbal answer they already delivered. A contradiction may mean they don't want to say what they feel inside, or it may mean they have two answers with equal importance. The prospect may have a part of them that is wholeheartedly saying, "Yes", and a part of them saying, "No". A prospect may say "yes and no" in the following ways:

Yes, I want to buy a new car...
No, I do not want to spend the money.

Yes, I want to improve or upgrade his equipment...

No, I don't want to go through the hassle of installation.

Yes, I want to buy a new, larger house...
No, I am dreading the process of moving.

There are often two sides to a question or statement. In your backtrack, it is essential to answer, or pace, both sides. Most of the time what people say (what we consider to be the major part of the communication) is at the level of conscious awareness. It is at the unconscious level that the counter argument may exist. If you acknowledge only the conscious side, the unconscious side is still there and may eventually cause problems. <u>Handling the unconscious objection up front sets up part of the GREEN LIGHT mechanism.</u>

Pros and cons are a part of human nature and are expressed in almost every statement or question. If you only answer one side of their question, the other unanswered side makes itself known eventually. The prospect may not do this to you consciously. They may do it later covertly, after you think you have closed the sale. If these unspoken objections are ignored while you are selling, then at the close the person may say, "I have to ask my wife," or "I want to think about it. Check with me tomorrow.' Tomorrow he is not available and a week later you find out he has installed another salesperson's system. Those counter-examples that did not surface were still there, unsatisfied. If you don't get both pieces of their objection backtracked in a single utterance, the prospect will keep popping back and forth from one objection to another like a seesaw. If you do not handle that seesaw, the customer will most likely buy from someone else who seems to more completely understand and satisfy their needs.

Avoid Using REASON And WHY
Avoid using the words REASON and WHY when backtracking. It was suggested in Chapter 2 that you delete the word WHY from your sales vocabulary. Most prospects respond defensively to the words WHY and REASON when you use them in a backtrack. They feel that they have to defend their position, which is not good for rapport. You might substitute "I know you have a positive intention for wanting this, could you please tell me more about it?' instead.

IF
There was an old school of thought that anyone willing to look at

both sides of the situation rather than taking a firm stand was being wish-washy and lacking in integrity. While that may be true in some contexts, the **Green Light Selling** model shows it is to your advantage to listen to every utterance that comes out of your prospect's mouth and pace both sides in your response. That is the purpose of adding the word **IF** in your backtrack; "So, **IF** I understand you correctly..."The **IF** says in a sense I *do* understand, and in a sense I *do not* understand. Other words that say this are: could, can, possible, might, or may. Sentences with these words in them usually are linguistically pacing both sides of an issue. Just a little practice with these words helps you develop one of the important skills top sales performers use every day.

BACKTRACK WITH ELBOW ROOM

> **"Our perceptions are only limited by our reality"**
> -Michael L. Phillips

In a backtrack, you can repeat back the words that the client said (word for word), you can rephrase it into your words, or you can rephrase it. There are times when a simple backtrack is not sufficient. If your prospect has given you a specification you know is difficult or impossible to meet, you need some additional maneuvering to bring your product/service back into acceptance range by adding an element of flexibility. As a master communicator, you can help your customer shift logical levels and assist them in finding more ways to meet their needs by backtracking with elbowroom.

Practice Your Creative Response

In structuring your backtrack, practice using your creativity and flair. Allow yourself to stretch your creative responses. No matter how difficult the requirements or how uncooperative the customer, assume the stance that they are saying nice things to you, even if they are not. Your creative replays give you more "Elbowroom" when dealing with your client. Even if they are indicating "No," you can still work toward a "Yes."

> Prospect: "Your company has a terrible reputation. There is no way I will do business with your company."

Your Creative Reply: "You want to make sure any company you do business with has a roster of satisfied, repeat customers."

Creative Stress Response Exercise

I started practicing my creative replies in a stressful situation so that my responses would become automatic in a similar stressful sales situation. It is an easy and fun exercise you can do while driving. For example, I practice my creative replies while driving down the highway in response to other drivers who insist on expressing their "excessive creativity behind the wheel." You know who I'm talking about, the folks who do a quick 3-lane shift in front of you to an exit or a variety of other really unusual and unexpected things.

I used to say things out loud or in my mind that were less than complimentary to these people. With practice, I have now forced my brain to make nice stories about these drivers. Here are some examples:

- "What an adventurous devil-may-care-person."
- "Look at how well their reflexes work, they did that without hitting anyone."
- "Incredible. Amazing acuity."

Now, my new response is automatic. Besides developing one's ability for "creative backtracking," this exercise has another side benefit. I used to hear other drivers yelling at me in my mind when I would have to execute a similarly stupid/creative maneuver with my car. Now, when I have to make my own "creative driving maneuvers," in my mind I now hear them say NICE things about my driving skills too!

> **Find a stressful situation where you find it hard to say nice things about people. Practice your creative replies and this skill will transfer to your sales repertoire.**

You can often enlarge the frame (jargon) of your prospect's requirements using a backtrack with elbowroom. However, if you try to get too much elbow room, you could risk losing rapport. So, watch the non-verbal signs that your prospect is giving. This is where sensory acuity comes in to make sure you are not going beyond what they are comfortable with. Here are some examples that show the difference between a simple backtrack and a backtrack with elbowroom.

PROSPECT: "We must have delivery by Thursday."

SIMPLE BACKTRACK: "So, you want to have it arrive at your office on or before Thursday of this week."

BACKTRACK WITH ELBOWROOM: "So, availability in the very near future is important to you."
In this example, "very near future" gives you more ways to handle the situation than Thursday. There is only one way to deliver on Thursday ... deliver on Thursday! There are probably several ways to deliver in the very near future ... depending upon how you define time.

PROSPECT: "It's too expensive."

SIMPLEBACKTRACK: "So, money is a definite issue."

BACKTRACK WITH ELBOWROOM: "So you need to make sure that you can budget for this."

PROSPECT: "But you don't have the color I want in stock."

SIMPLE BACKTRACK: "Having a specific color available now is important?"

BACKTRACK WITH ELBOWROOM: "So, both availability and coordination with your color scheme are important?"

PROSPECT: "I don't have time to go to the seminar."

SIMPLE BACKTRACK: "You're too busy to attend."

BACKTRACK WITH ELBOWROOM: "So, you want to make sure that your time is spent efficiently."
If you get a verbal or non-verbal "yes" to your backtrack, you know you were successful in your bid for elbow room. If you get a "no" answer, that means that you need to backtrack again using different words. You do not know how much elbow room you can get until you make the attempt. Using the process of backtracking with elbowroom makes it possible to achieve the following kind of flexibility:

"Must be IBM compatible" ... can become ... "Able to be used with current equipment."

"Costs less than $2000" ... can become ... "Fits within your budget."

"5-year guaranteed life" ... can become ... "Assurance of continued productivity."

"Cancellation clause" ... can become ... "Adequate post-contract flexibility."

If your prospect does not agree with your backtrack, continue asking for more information about the requirement until you can state a backtrack in words that meet your prospect's complete satisfaction. A successful backtrack with elbowroom gives you more latitude in answering your prospect's requirements. This is to your advantage later, when you are demonstrating how your product's features match the client's requirements.

Be Consistent
A backtrack with elbowroom is a way of shifting your prospect's requirements from **what they say they want -** to additional **ways you can fill those needs.** If you use this process on all requirements, even if you can supply that specification, it forms a pattern to your selling that is consistent and easy for your prospects to follow. Human brains learn quickly and usually require only two or three examples to discern a pattern of behavior. Many times learning is acquired through only one experience. Forming a pattern in your selling that remains consistent makes it easy for your prospects to follow and understand what you are saying.

Example 1
Your prospect says: "I don't have the authority to do that."

A Little Elbowroom: "This is not your department, this issue exceeds your authority."

A Little More Elbowroom: "You want to make sure you do not encroach on other people's area of responsibility."

A Lot of Elbowroom: "So, you can only help me identify the people who are responsible for this."

Example 2
Your prospect says: "I really want to do this, but I don't know if the timing is right yet."

One-word backtrack: "Timing."
(Select a word they say and repeat it back to them. It indicates to them that you heard the whole thing.)

A More Complete Backtrack: "So, even if you want to do it, timing is important."

A Little Elbowroom: "So, you will only do this if you both want it - and the timing fits your schedule."

A Lot of Elbowroom: "So, you're trying to satisfy many things within a tight schedule."

Linguistic Softeners
Sometimes it is necessary to use qualifiers to avoid offending people's belief systems. Linguistic softeners are an attempt to make sure you have not over-generalized. Even if you are 100% sure that you have the best product ... you still should say, "Many people feel that our product is superior to the majority of the products in the marketplace." Softeners are qualifiers such as: More or less, Kind of, etc. They keep you from locking yourself down too tightly.

These are a few softening words and phrases that can be used to describe your product or service:
- sometimes
- some people say
- you may have noticed
- perhaps
- there is a sense in which
- one way to think about this is
- if what we claim is true
- if you accept the basic premise
- a majority of the time
- you will almost certainly find
- you can realistically expect
- the evidence suggests
- we have developed confidence in

CONDITIONAL CLOSE

After an effective backtrack, you are ready to use a conditional close. A conditional close goes like this: *"If we can meet those requirements, is there going to be anything else you require?"* You backtrack until you get the non-verbal and verbal confirmation that what you said to the prospect means the same (to them) as what they said to you. You also use the conditional close to help get out all of the customer's requirements. This helps later when you do your presentation. Then you are able to match your product or service to what the customer has stated as their requirements.

So, after a successful backtrack, you do a conditional close, using questions similar to the ones listed below.

> "If we can handle those color issues, is there anything else you require?"

> "If we can meet those requirements to your complete and total satisfaction, is there anything else you need?"

> "So, if I could demonstrate that X would be taken care of, then you would be interested in this proposal. Is that correct?"

Remember, if your prospects do not agree with your backtrack / conditional close, continue asking for more information about the requirement until you can state it to their complete satisfaction.

Examples Of A Backtrack Followed By A Conditional Close:

> PROSPECT: "I need _____ "

> BACKTRACK WITH ELBOW ROOM: "If I understand correctly, you want to _____ "

> PROSPECT: "That's right."

> CONDITIONAL CLOSE: "If we can meet those requirements, is there anything else you need?"

> PROSPECT: "I need a calculator that has a printer and is powered by sunlight."

BACKTRACK WITH ELBOW ROOM: "If I understand correctly, you want to have hard copy and avoid the cost of batteries."

PROSPECT: "That's right."

CONDITIONAL CLOSE: "If we can meet those requirements, is there anything else you need?"

PROSPECT: "I need a 3-cycle dishwasher that has a pots and pans cycle and will fit in my kitchen."

BACKTRACK WITH ELBOWROOM: "If I understand correctly, you want a dishwasher that will adequately clean your dishes and fit in your kitchen."

PROSPECT: "That's right."

CONDITIONAL CLOSE: "If we can meet those requirements, is there anything else you need?"

Learning to use backtracking and conditional close techniques will allow you to elicit your prospect's buying procedure more elegantly.

Points To Remember
1. SHIFT LOGICAL LEVELS TO MAKE MORE OPTIONS AVAILABLE TO YOUR CLIENT.
2. USE BACKTRACKING TO ACKNOWLEDGE WHAT THE CUSTOMER HAS SAID.
3. BACKTRACK WITH ELBOW ROOM TO EXPAND THE WAYS TO MEET YOUR CUSTOMER"S REQUIREMENTS.
4. USE CONDITIONAL CLOSE TO ELICIT THE REST OF THE CUSTOMER'S REQUIREMENTS.

Chapter 6

LET THEM HELP YOU MAKE THE SALE

Using the tools of BACKTRACK and CONDITIONAL CLOSE that you learned in the last chapter, you can now discover the customer's buying procedure. With their BUYING PROCEDURE in hand, the lights are all starting to turn GREEN!

My old Ford chugged and stopped. The time to buy a new car was definitely here. Once I had decided to buy a car, I checked out three companies for a price comparison. At noon, I drove down to the Anderson Ford company, picked out the car I wanted, came to an agreement on price with the salesman, and went back to work. I bought this car the same way I bought the last one and the one before that.

The housewife making a cake gets the bowl out of the cupboard, the beater from the drawer, and the cake mix from the pantry. She walks around her kitchen assembling ingredients in the same basic pattern she has followed many times.

The airline pilot straps himself into his seat, puts on his headgear, and goes through the safety checklist. Before he moves the plane, he does the same things he has done hundreds of times before. He has an established method for preparing to fly.

The runner preparing to race sits on the ground, stretches her legs, and then moves to stretching other parts of her body. While she is doing this, she conditions herself mentally for the task ahead.

In each of these examples, the individual has performed the task at hand so many times that they have become systematic in their behavior. Being systematic allows them to repeat things they have already done before in the fastest manner.

Procedures Are A Way Of Life

> **"Habit is stronger than reason."**
> -George Santayana

Developing patterns of behavior is natural for all of us. Consider your time at home and work. You almost certainly have an established system for doing many activities and may have a procedure for almost everything you do. Once you have determined the optimal way to successfully complete an activity, you have developed a procedure for doing that particular job. Following the procedure essentially becomes an operating habit. In the same way, our prospects generally use the same procedure or strategies for buying that they have been successful with in the past. Eliciting your prospect's buying procedure (strategy) starts by asking a question such as: "What method have you used in the past to successfully make this kind of decision?"

Know Your Client's Buying Strategy

Knowing your prospect's buying strategy - learning how to do things their way - has many advantages for you and them. First, it tells them you are willing to serve them on their terms. You are able to help them buy your product in the manner which is absolutely the most comfortable for them. Second, it also helps you to determine if they are willing to form a contract of intention to buy if certain conditions are met. Figure I on the next page shows a sample of a typical buying strategy.

Following is a typical buying procedure showing the conditions that need to be satisfied to move forward. In this example of a salesperson selling a computer system, the prospect's buying strategy flows like this:

FIRST CONDITION: If they have enough curiosity, THEN
ACTION STEP: They will evaluate their current system;
THEN

SECOND CONDITION: If their current system seems deficient enough, THEN
ACTION STEP: They will poll their company for new needs;
THEN

THIRD CONDITION: If enough needs exist, THEN
ACTION STEP: They will prepare a request for proposals;
THEN

FOURTH CONDITION: If the proposals are responsive enough, THEN
ACTION STEP: They will evaluate them; THEN

FIFTH CONDITION: If one is good enough, THEN
ACTION STEP: They will select a successful vendor; THEN

SIXTH CONDITION: If the proposed contract is good enough, THEN
ACTION STEP: THEN THEY WILL BUY.

- **Discovering your prospect's buying procedures is best done with an attitude that says, "I want to know your process so I can better serve you. "**

You begin by asking: "What is your procedure for_____ ?" or "What method do you use for deciding to _____? or "How would you know to buy _____?"

Your prospects may not have consciously thought about their methods for buying the product or service you are offering. Your questions will cause them to think about how they go through their buying process time after time. As soon as a prospect begins giving you an answer, begin writing it down. Writing your prospect's procedure on paper does these things:
- It tells them you are serious about serving their company.
- It shows you are considerate of their standard method for doing things.
- It helps you remember the steps.
This is essential. You want to sell to your prospects their way; using the steps of their personal procedures.

After they respond, you acknowledge their first answer, and encourage them to give the next step in their procedure by saying, "What would be your next step?" or "Then what would you do?" or simply "And then?"

After you have been given three or four steps of their buying procedure, you backtrack, listing all the steps you have so far, and do a conditional close. "If we can do_____ satisfactorily, what is next?" There may or may not be another step. If there is not, they will tell you. If there is, continue by backtracking that step. When you think you have all the steps, you backtrack the whole procedure and do a conditional close.

64

After you have gained some experience eliciting buying procedures from several of your customers, you develop a sense of knowing whether your prospects have mentioned all the things they need to consider before buying. If they leave out an issue that your experience has taught you is an issue for the majority of your prospects, you can bring that in with a backtrack, watching to see if there is agreement.

- **IMPORTANT: Everyone has their own buying procedure that is unique to them. Never assume that "what works for one individual works for everyone." You must take the time to uncover the buying strategy for each customer. Don't skip steps!**

If a buying strategy flows, it steers the customer into a natural "yes-buy-now" decision. This is the normal motivational flow for this customer's decision making, and the result means a sale for you.

Basic Format For Eliciting Procedure:
- **SALESPERSON: "What is your procedure for____?"**
- **PROSPECT: "I need_____."(3 or 4 examples)**
- **SALESPERSON" Backtrack and conditional close.**
- **PROSPECT: "Final step."**
- **SALESPERSON: Backtrack and conditional close.**

Ambivalence
As you elicit your prospect's buying procedure, you will probably notice the pro and con (yes/no) phenomena mentioned earlier surfacing in what they say. This opposition seems to cause a certain amount of ambivalence to appear in almost every statement or question.

For example, if you ask your prospect, *"What is your procedure for buying an air purifier?"* The person may say,

"Well, first I have to decide if one would help me to feel better." There is a part of your prospect that says, *"Breathing clean air would make me more healthy,"* and another part that questions, *"Would it really?"* The no part sends out a charge that lights up a red light. The yes part sends out a charge that lights up a green light. Each step in your customer's buying procedure carries this charge. You are not interested in any steps that say no. You are only interested in

following the yes charges ... these are called GREEN LIGHTS.

We are introducing a prospect, taken from a real life example, so that you may more fully understand how the **Green Light Selling** model works. He will make his entrance here and accompany us throughout the remainder of the book. His name is Boyd, and he is calling to learn about a sales training being offered.

THE MODEL IN ACTION

Note: (See Chapter 7 for more information on Criteria Words and Phrases)

Boyd Enters

DON: "Thank you for calling Alter Dynamics. This is Don. May I help you?"

BOYD: "Yes. I'm calling about the sales training you are offering."

DON: "Excellent. May I ask, please, who is calling?"

BOYD: "My name is Boyd Smith."

DON: "Thank you for calling, Boyd. How did you find out about our training?" **(Checking for relationship.)**

BOYD: "Tom Baker told me about it. He went to a seminar you had in New York a few months ago."

DON: "Yes. I remember Tom. He is a sharp guy; nice to work with and learns quickly. How did you meet Tom, Boyd?" **(Relationship question-referral.)**

BOYD: "I've known him a long time, for 5 or 6 years. I sell for Interstate Range, and we cross paths every so often. He is a great guy to be around. We always have a lot of fun, and that helps me unwind. I saw him last in Salt Lake City a couple of weeks ago. That's when he told me about your class. **(Fun and unwind are criteria words.)**

DON: "Boyd, if I understand correctly, you have gained quite a bit of interest in this sales class. What would be your procedure, Boyd, for deciding whether or not you would take this training?" **(Asking for procedure or buying strategy.)**

BOYD: "There are a lot of important factors I would need to consider before I agree to sign up for it."

DON: "So, you would want to make sure you have considered all the important factors before you make this kind of decision? Is that correct?" **(Simple backtrack.)**

BOYD: "That's right."

DON: "Can you tell me one of the factors that you are considering?"

BOYD: "Well, one of them is just the nature of what I do. I don't want to book myself into something too far in advance, because when I attend training it often comes up at the last minute, which is a challenge. Really what I'd like to do is, a couple of days before the training starts decide if I can definitely go and just take off and do it. " **(Challenge is another criteria word.)**

DON: "So, next, you would want to make sure that you had an appropriate degree of flexibility for attendance." **(Backtrack with elbow room.)**

BOYD: "That sounds about right. I want to be able to pick up the phone 2 days before the training and say, 'Hey, I'm coming in. I want to take this training, and I'll bring a check.'"

DON: "If I understand correctly, Boyd, if it's at all possible you want to retain flexibility for attendance." **(Leveraged outcome.)**

BOYD: "Correct." **(Green light.)**

DON: "If we could make sure that you retain _t7exibility for attendance, is there anything else that you would require?" **(Conditional close.)**

BOYD: "Well, I would want to make sure that the class was

worth the time invested." **(Criteria phrase.)**

DON: "So, as a person who understands the value of time, and knows how to use it properly, you want to be certain that what you are learning is worth the time invested." **(Backtrack.)**

BOYD: "That's right." **(Green light.)**

DON: "If you were satisfied that this class was worth the time invested, is there anything else you would require?"

BOYD: "Well, I do have a cost consideration, too." **(Criteria phrase.)**

DON: "So you want to make sure that this is within your budgets" **(Backtrack with elbow room.)**

BOYD: "Yes. A lot depends on whether or not I make a minimum of $3,500 between now and next month."

DON: "So, as a prudent money manager, and a person who wants to make sure he can meet all of his financial obligations, you would want to make sure your cost consideration is met before you would actually attend the class?"

BOYD: "Yes, I'd attend the class, as long as I had made the $3,500." **(This answer requires additional handling, which will be discussed in the next chapter.)**

DON: "So, if you were absolutely satisfied that you had considered all the important factors, were able to retain flexibility for attendance, had decided this class was worth the time invested, and your cost consideration was met, then you would go ahead and 'do it'?"

BOYD: "That's right." **(We have the procedure and green lights all the way home.)**

Recap
The first three questions that Boyd was asked began to establish relationship. They are also questions that Boyd can answer. You want your prospect to feel comfortable and capable. Because it was a

friend who told Boyd about the class, you at least temporarily gain the relationship of that referral. From this interaction, you have established that Boyd's procedure for deciding to take a training class are:

- Consider all the important factors.
- Retain flexibility for attendance.
- Worth the time invested.
- Cost consideration met.
- "Do it."

Leveraging Their Procedure

Once you have your prospect's procedures in writing and they agree that the words used to state their procedure are correct, you have in effect established a contract; they have agreed that if their specific conditions are met they will buy. This gives you leverage that can be used later if they attempt to add an additional step. If they should attempt to bring in another step, you would use the leverage by saying, "Excuse me. I thought you said that_____. Is that not correct?" If they say, "Yes, that's correct," you move on. If they say, "No," you say, "Oh, excuse me for getting it wrong." Then you throw away the paper that has the procedure written on it and begin again by going through the process of eliciting their procedure.

POINTS TO REMEMBER-
1. ELICIT THE CUSTOMER'S BUYING PROCEDURE
2. PACE BOTH SIDES OF YOUR CUSTOMER'S STATEMENTS AND QUESTIONS
3. GET THE BUYING PROCEDURE IN WRITING SO YOU CAN HAVE GREEN LIGHTS ALL THE WAY HOME
4. BACKTRACK AND LEVERAGE THEIR PROCEDURE

Chapter 7

Yesterday, my patience was rapidly draining away. The salesman sitting across from me was so caught up in explaining the features of his product, that he was not listening to what I was saying. I kept looking at my watch, thinking of graceful ways to excuse myself.

Today, I had an appointment with one of his competitors. This salesman listened as I explained what I specifically wanted for my computer operation. His attentiveness helped me see more clearly what I really needed.

NEEDS VS. WANTS AND SPECIFICATIONS

What a customer actually needs is usually out of their conscious awareness. Real needs have a tendency to get lost or confused in what people "think" they want and in unnecessary specifications.

For example, your customer may come in with their minds set on buying a specific product (which we'll call "X'). They may have recently read about X, and will probably give you a list of their "X-like" wants and specifications. Don't be alarmed that X isn't in your product line. They don't really want X, they need what X can do for them. Once you can discover and define your prospect's actual needs (what X will do for them), you can satisfy the customer with an appropriate product/service.

It has been aptly said, " You sell them what they want, and give them what they need." Your first job as a salesperson is to help your prospects clarify the difference between their needs (what actually must be accomplished or satisfied) and their needs specifications (the customer's best guess of how to get their NEED met). Everyone has needs. Generally, you will find that all people have the same basic needs: food, safety, love (belonging), and social approval. The particular way each person has of satisfying their needs is called a specification.

A Want (Specification) Is Not Always A Need

Your client may say they NEED a late model Taurus station wagon with 4-wheel drive. What they have actually given you is a specification or a "possible" way that their actual need(s) can be met.

70

The unexpressed need behind the Taurus station wagon (specification) might be transportation, status, mobility, or convenience. Therefore, the client's need can probably be accomplished with several different vehicles or options.

- **A specification does not define what the need really is.**

Think of your customer as a person needing to have their tax return prepared and yourself (the salesperson) as the tax consultant. When you walk into the customer's office, he is a stranger with a shoebox filled with unorganized receipts.

While you know absolutely nothing about what his shoebox contains (specifications), you know the structure necessary to help him finalize his tax return (his need). Your job (as the tax consultant) is to get the data organized for this customer.

The customer may say, "Why don't you dump all that stuff (wants and specifications) in the middle of my desk and we'll sort through it." Instead, you suggest looking for receipts for each entry that must be filled in to complete the tax return (his need). You ask for interest payments, bank statements, business deductions, etc. Before long, you've been through the whole box translating the client's wants and specifications (receipts) into entries on the form and a completed tax return (his real need).

As a tax consultant, it was your job to organize the receipts in the shoe box in a relevant way so that the tax return could be completed. In a similar fashion, your job in sales is to translate the customer's wants and specifications into needs that best satisfies them. Through this organizational process, both the salesperson's and customer's outcomes can be achieved.

> **"One of the best ways to persuade others is with your ears, by listening to them."**
> -Dean Rusk

While it is not always possible for you to meet the client's specifications, his needs must always be satisfied. If you cannot satisfy the customer's actual needs, they will search for someone who can. However, if you can translate their specifications and wants into their actual need, it is easy for the customer to understand how your product or service matches those needs. Criteria words are an excellent way to make that translation.

CRITERIA WORDS

Words are the primary way we have of labeling objects and describing events. Everyone understands words like horse, chair, or table, which describe concrete objects. These words have the same general meaning (definition) to everyone. However, other kinds of words are used to describe subjective experiences. These are criteria words. Words such as *happiness, uniqueness, or affordability* have different meanings to everyone who uses them. People use these criteria words to describe the way they feel about themselves, others, things in their life, and events going on around them.

Criteria words are as varied, endless, and changing as people and their circumstances. The specific criteria words individuals use to describe their wants and needs are of particular importance to them. The following list shows a small sample of some commonly used criteria words and phrases you hear people use.

Common Criteria Words

Loving, Caring, Sincere, New, Different, Same as, Smart, Intelligent, Familiar, Reasonable, Interesting, Productive, Cozy, Warm, Cool

When people hear these words and other phrases, they create a picture, feel an emotion, or hear sounds that are closely associated with emotional experience they have had. When people hear or read these words, they have an involuntarily response which unconsciously returns them to the original experience that attached "the meaning" to the word or phrase.

Finding Your Own Criteria Words

An easy way for you to identify whether a word could be a criteria word for you is to ask yourself this question: "Do I know what this word means?' If the word does not have an exact meaning, it could be a criteria word. For example: A 10' by 12' room is the same for everyone, but a cozy room is a matter of interpretation. A black Model-T Ford is the same for everyone, but there are many classic cars available.

The fact that people will tell you their criteria words (they tend to pop up repeatedly in their conversation) is extremely important to you. Once you have correctly identified your prospect's criteria words, you can describe the features of your product or service in words that are meaningful to them. It's like creating a personalized advertisement tailored just for that individual. If you can use their criteria words to describe the features of your product or service, and if what you sell fills their needs, you have an 85% plus chance of closing the sale.

- **People love to hear their own criteria words. In fact, they never tire of hearing their own words and thoughts.**

An Example Of Using Criteria Words:

Suppose you are a car salesman and your prospect is looking at a new Ford station wagon. He makes the following statement, "It reminds me of a station wagon I once owned that was real **economical**. And it looks big enough for all the kids to be **comfortable**. I wonder if it would be as **dependable** as my other wagon."

His criteria words could be *economical, comfortable, and dependable.* If you pay attention to his non-verbal behavior as he vocalizes his criteria words, the customer may highlight his criteria words with a change in voice tone. He could also raise his eyebrows or add a hand gesture to emphasize his "special words." Tune into your prospect's words and actions. Then, watch closely as you repeat the words back to them in your normal conversation. Notice if they seem to access an emotional state when hearing the criteria words. What you are looking for is if the customer becomes more attentive or involved. If so, those select words are likely to be their criteria words.

Another way of checking is to repeat the customer's statement back to them and substitute a different word in place of what you suspect is their criteria word.

Example: "So you think that car looks interesting." If he looks at you blankly and says, 'No, comfortable." You can be absolutely certain that comfortable is one of his criteria words. In this example, once you have correctly identified your prospect's criteria words, you know he is likely to buy a car that he perceives as economical, comfortable, and dependable.

Uncovering Criteria Words
To discover a person's criteria words, it is often acceptable to ask information gathering questions such as:

"What criteria are you using to make this decision?"

"What are you trying to accomplish by this action?"

"What does having that do for you?"

To find the customer's criteria words for a specific type of action, product, or service, you can use the following basic format of questions. Fill in the blank with whatever is appropriate to what you sell. These types of questions will receive specific information:

"What do you like about_____?"

"What will _____ do for you?"

For more information, you can ask questions such as:

"What does having that do for you?"

"What does having that really do for you?"

Using the Word *Really*
The word really has a tendency to cause people to dig deeper into their standard list of labels for important internal feelings and descriptions.

Example: "I know you find this class exciting, but how do you really justify the time and expense?"

Response: "Well, you know ... it's important to know what's new and protect yourself from getting behind on things that could impact your career." (New, protect, and impact are words that describe more internal feelings.)

Other Methods
"As If" and "Shifting Reference"

You can often elicit criteria words indirectly by using the AS IF frame or by SHIFTING REFERENCE. To use the AS IF frame, you ask the person to imagine something from a future point of view.

Examples:

"Provided this decision turns out to be successful, what will be the most important payoffs you will be experiencing a year from now?"

"When you do receive that large tax return, how will that change your lifestyle?"

Using the SHIFTING REFERENCE technique enables the person to take someone else's point of view.

Examples:

"If people you know who are good at these kinds of decisions were here, what would they say are the most important things we should be considering at this time?"

"If your sales manager was here today, what do you think he would want from you?"

As you develop your sensory acuity (your ability to notice people's unconscious responses by shifts in facial expressions, voice tones, body postures, etc.), you will recognize people's criteria words by noticing their responses to specific words as they are saying them, or as they hear these words being said to them. With a little practice, you will remember criteria words easily. You could also carry a small pad and pencil and write criteria words and phrases down for later reference.

Don't Translate Criteria Words

It is important to use your prospect's criteria words exactly as they say them and not to modify them in any way! Remember that all people have their own significant meaning for the words they say. If you translate your prospect's words into another form, they are no longer their criteria words. For example:

Performed is not the same as *performing*;

Smart buy is not the same as *good buy*;

Comforting is not the same as *comfortable.*

If you try to translate a customer's criteria word(s), they have to translate your words back into their experience to create meaning. Translating a customer's criteria words loses the sparkle and appeal much as losing carbonation makes root beer flat.

Let's revisit our prospect, Boyd, and see how using his criteria words can make a difference. (At this point, you may want to reread the first interaction with Boyd in Chapter 6, to see how his initial criteria words were discovered.)

THE MODEL IN ACTION
Boyd Re-Enters

> DON: "So, if you were absolutely satisfied that you had considered all the important factors, were able to retain flexibility for attendance, had decided this class was worth the time invested, and your cost consideration was met, then you would go ahead and 'do it'." **(Green lights set.)**
>
> BOYD: "That's right."
>
> DON. "Boyd, if I understand correctly, you have gained quite a bit of interest in this sales class. What would you expect to get out of a training of this sort?"
>
> BOYD: "I'd like to make more money. I could do that if I closed more of my sales. I'm getting about one out of four right now. Tom told me he is now closing three or four out of every five. Odds like that would sure reduce the stress of this profession."
>
> DON: "So, if I understand fully, you would like to make more money and reduce the stress. Is there anything else you want?" **(Backtracking criteria phrases.)**
>
> BOYD: "Well, Tom looked real good when I saw him last. He had this kind of confident glow about him, like he could meet any challenge. I would like to have that."
>
> DON: "If you had that confident glow, Boyd, what would that do for you?" **(Asking for deeper criteria.)**
>
> BOYD: "I would be able to walk into any business in any town and meet people on their ground. I would be able to pick the right words, depending on the mood of the person I am talking to, and I would not get flustered like I sometimes do now. "

DON: "So, if I understand correctly what you are saying, you would like to avoid getting flustered to the point where you would have that confident glow like Tom has, so you could walk into any business in town that you normally go into, and no matter the situation, say the right words to meet people on their own ground. Is that what you would like to do?" **(Backtracking criteria phrases.)**

BOYD: "That's right. I guess what I really want is to be a top notch salesman. I do all right, but sometimes I walk into a place, and maybe the boss is in a bad mood and wants to take it out on me, or else he is in a good mood and wants to talk. Either way, I lose control of the situation. I would like to be able to get through the presentation without losing track of myself."

Summary
You have discovered that FUN, UNWIND, MAKE MORE MONEY, REDUCE THE STRESS, CONFIDENT GLOW, and CHALLENGE may be some of Boyd's criteria words. You have also discovered what he wants out of training. You could now make a list of his needs.
- Make more money.
- Reduce the stress.
- Be a top notch salesman.
- Meet people on their own ground.
- Pick the right words.
- Avoid getting flustered.
- Control the situation.

The next step in the selling process is to learn what to do with Boyd's needs.

POINTS TO PEMEMBER-

1. KNOW THE DIFFERENCE BETWEEN YOUR CLIENT'S NEEDS AND WANTS OR SPECIFICATIONS
2. YOUR PROSPECT'S NEEDS MUST BE MET
3. DESIGN QUESTIONS TO HELP IDENTIFY YOUR CUSTOMER'S CRITERIA WORDS
4. USE THE AS IF AND SHIFTING REFERENCE AS ANOTHER METHOD OF DISCOVERING CRITERIA
5. DON"T TRANSLATE YOUR CUSTOMER"S CRITERIA WORDS, USE THEM VERBATIM

Chapter 8

"There is no such thing as 'soft sell' and 'hard sell.' There is only 'smart sell' and 'stupid sell'."
-Charles Brower

I walked in the door and straight to the kitchen, intent on a cold drink, a soft chair, and something to prop my feet up. My mind continued to focus on the sales presentation I had given today. It had been a good one. I had covered all the facts and relevant data. The committee was sold except for Jack Applegate. He was still holding out for his 'idealized' computer system.

My wife kissed me on the cheek and greeted me with "Hi honey, I have supper about ready. As soon as we eat, we can go."

I stifled a groan. I had forgotten our plans to go dancing tonight. After being on my feet all day, dancing was about the last thing I wanted to do. "Honey," I asked carefully, "Do you really want to go dancing tonight?"

She gave me a long look before she smiled. "I don't care if we go dancing or take a walk or just sit on the porch. What I really want is for us to spend some time together."

Something clicked in my brain. What she had previously asked for was not what she really wanted. In my mind, I kept seeing Jack Applegate asking for those impossible specifications. He knew there was not a computer system built that had those kind of capabilities. What did he really want? Tomorrow, I would find out.

GOING BEYOND CRITERIA

In a sales situation, a closure is considered successful when the salesperson's **OUTCOMES** are met by filling the prospect's **NEEDS**. Your client may be adamant about having gold trim on his day-timer, but what if that is too costly or impossible to provide? When prospects give specifications that are difficult or impossible to handle, it is important to remember that beneath their seemingly impossible requests are real needs that must be satisfied. What happens when you cannot find the need behind their specification? What happens when you cannot supply a specification that the client "will not do without?"

- **Once you get to intent, you can close on the objection.**

While a **backtrack with elbow room** or discovering **criteria words** may give you some insight, there are times when a client's actual needs are deeply buried. In this case, to uncover the customer's needs you must use a more powerful probing process to uncover the **intent** behind the prospect's request. The process of Outframing helps you get to their intent and allows you to find a way to satisfy the hidden need.

OUTFRAMING TO GET TO INTENT

The process of outframing creates a different viewpoint, much like enlarging the frame on a picture. Suppose you were looking at a picture of a tree in a very small frame. Enlarging the frame would show you that the tree was surrounded by other trees and was really part of a forest. Moving the frame out even farther shows that the forest is surrounded by large rock cliffs and is part of a mountain range. Outframing shifts logical levels and gives you more flexibility to discover what the client is trying to accomplish so you can satisfy their intent (need).

- **Outframing shows the customer a bigger picture.**

Say your client is determined to have purple stripes, but your product isn't manufactured that way. You could retool to manufacture the product to supply the purple stripes, but the cost would be so high you would no longer be competitive. Purple stripes are not a **need** because *no one really needs purple stripes!* Now, you still want to service this customer and make the sale. You must discover the intent for the purple stripes before you can make the sale. Why are these purple stripes are so important to the client? What need do they fill?

- **Using an outframe moves the customer from wanting a single specification to accepting a broader image of specifications that can also meet their need.**

Outframing Method

The OUTFRAME is accomplished by asking a carefully constructed question to uncover the basic need that has remained hidden. The format goes like this:

> **"I know you have some positive intention for wanting
> _____. I'm not sure exactly what it is. Can you please
> tell me more about that?"**

The only time an outframe will not work is when you honestly should not be dealing with the client in the first place. That could be a pre-qualification problem. (We will discuss this facet in a later chapter.)

Examples

"I understand that your company has certain procedures and guidelines that you need to follow in order to implement something of this nature. Could you fill me in a little bit more on the specifics and what you need as far as prices and specific training skills that you would need your salesmen equipped with?"

"I know you have some positive intention for wanting to buy a quality water heater for $150.00. I'm not 100% clear in my mind what you are trying to accomplish. What is that?"

"I know there is some important function to be served with this requirement. What is it?"

"I know you are trying to accomplish something of value by changing your logo color. What is it?"

Conversational Outframing - How It Works

Suppose your customer is looking for a hand-held video camcorder that *runs on D-cell batteries* - a specification you do not sell. You don't know why they want this specific capability and their criteria words haven't given you a clue either. If you can discover the customer's intent for needing this one specification, you can easily direct the customer to other camcorders which you do have in stock and would adequately meet their needs.

So you ask: "I know you have some positive intention for wanting a video camcorder that runs on D-cell batteries. I'm not sure exactly what it is. Can you please tell me more about that?"

You discover that the prospect is going to Europe and needs a camcorder that does not require U.S. electrical current to operate or recharge its batteries. Having this information, you can sell him a camcorder that works on both European and U.S. electrical current. The use of electricity was not an objection. The compatibility with different types of electricity was.

Suppose your spouse has told you that they want to go to a "particular" movie this evening. You don't know why that specific movie appeals to your spouse, but you don't particularly care for the movie's stars or subject matter. By outframing to shift logical levels, you can discover the intent behind the desire to attend the specific movie. So you ask: "I know you have some positive intention for wanting to go see that particular movie. I'm not sure exactly what it is. Can you please tell me what about it appeals to you?"

You may discover that your spouse feels stressed and needs to relax. The thought of going to see a comedy seemed to them like an appealing way to unwind. Knowing that information, you can explore other options that both partners find more appealing as a way to unwind and relax.

Have You Moved To Intent?
Try this simple test to see if your **OUTFRAME** has shifted logical levels from a specification to the intent (need) behind it.

Specification - - - -to - - - Intent

Ask yourself, "Is this something I would need?"

A camcorder that runs on batteries is a **specification.** Compatibility with European electric current is a need (that you must satisfy).

Going to a show would not necessarily fill a need for you. Relaxing or unwinding probably would fill a need.

<u>Avoid The Words REASON, WHY, And BUT In Your Outframe Question</u>

"George, I know you have a reason for wanting to buy Woolie Looms. I'm not sure I understand why you want that specific product. But, I just don't understand, can you enlighten me a little bit more?"

This example carries all the do not's of outframing. Just as in backtracking, the word REASON elicits the same kind of response from your prospect as the word WHY. Asking the question using the words REASON and WHY puts people on the defensive. The word BUT has a tendency to cancel out the thought before it. Finally, when asking a question of importance, you don't want them to forget the premise of your question. A better OUTFRAME question would be:

"George, I know that buying only Woolie Looms is what you have preferred. Could you please explain to me what about this specific brand is so important to you?"

Examples Of Effective Outframes

Interior Decorator and Client:
CLIENT: "I like your ideas for improving this room. You can do everything you suggested except move the mural on the wall."

GET TO INTENT: "I know you must have a specific function in mind for wanting to keep this mural in place. I am not sure I know what it is. What are you trying to accomplish by leaving it where it is?"

CLIENT: "I want it to have an open and airy feeling in here." Now the decorator may be able to offer suggestions that get rid of the hideous mural on the wall and yet retain an open and airy feeling.

Sales Trainer and Company Sales Manager.
PROSPECT: "We are willing to spend $500 on this training.

GET TO INTENT: "I know that you have something of value that you want to accomplish for having quality training for only $500. I am not a 100 % clear in my own mind what you are trying to accomplish. Could you tell me what it is?"

PROSPECT: "Well, that is all the money left in the allotted budget for this year."

Now the sales trainer may be able to ask for the procedure for getting a supplementary training budget for this year.

TRANSLATE

As you learned your prospect's buying procedures, you discovered some of their criteria words. They will use many of those same words (and also some new ones) when they describe their intent to you. Both sets of criteria words are valuable to you ... because they hold emotional impact for your client. It is not necessary for you to know what the criteria words and phrases mean to them. You just have to know that the words are important to them and remember to use them throughout the selling process. It is also necessary in your backtrack for you to use the client's criteria words to label their need(s)/intent.

For example, remember the man who wanted a car that was roomy, dependable, and economical. You cannot know what emotional charge those words carry for him. It is enough to know that those words impact him emotionally to the extent that he will want to buy a car that he feels will be roomy, dependable, and economical.

- **Translating needs into criteria words gives you the balance of the information you need to prepare your presentation.**

Now, Don takes Boyd further through the **Green Light Selling model** and discovers Boyd's needs and intents. The example shows how Outframing can be used to expand the options available to the customer and also to further unearth the customer's needs.

THE MODEL IN ACTION
Boyd And The Unknown $3,500 Specification

In our first encounter with Boyd, we learned that his criteria words could be fun, unwind, and challenge. During the next phase we added these words: make more money, reduce the stress, confident glow, valuable, and flexibility. He said the word challenge twice. While he did not actually use the word flexible himself, he agreed with its use three times. These words will be noted and saved for later use. Next we return to our conversation with Boyd and discover what the underlying need is behind his desire to earn $3,500 in the next month.

DON: "I know that it is important for you to earn $3,500 between now and next month. I'm not sure I know exactly what the real need (intent) behind this is. What is the purpose of earning that exact amount?" **(Outframe)**

BOYD: "Well, I talked it over with my friend Joe, who is also my accountant. He said the amount I need to earn to pay my taxes next month and have the cash to pay for this training is $3,500."

DON: "So, as a prudent money manager and a person who wants to make sure he can meet all financial obligations, you would want to make sure your cash flow is appropriate before you would actually attend the class?" **(Backtrack with elbowroom.)**

BOYD: "Yes."

DON: "And once you have considered all the important factors in selecting a training, if you are able to retain flexibility for attendance, you decide it is worth the time invested and providing your cost considerations are Met, is there anything else you require before you tell yourself to 'do it'?" **(Conditional close.)**

BOYD: "That about covers it." **(Conditional close accepted.)**

DON: "Boyd, I'm not sure if our training is what you want or not. I do know how to find out. What I would like to do is get together so that we can determine if what we have to offer in this training will be valuable to you and present an appropriate challenge. It would take about 30 minutes of your time to show you some of the material we cover in this training and tell you some of the options that might be useful to you in learning to establish that confident glow. Is there a time in the near future when you could drop by the office so we could do that? I'm available Monday morning at 10:00 or 3:30 in the afternoon. "

BOYD: "Monday at 3:30 would work."

Note: We have organized Boyd's data in a manner that is understandable to him and makes it hard for him to say no to his own specifications.

MOVING ON

Now that you have your prospect's CRITERIA WORDS IN MIND (Chapter 5), you know how to obtain their PROCEDURE FOR BUYING YOUR PRODUCT OR SERVICE (Chapter 6). You have a CLEAR UNDERSTANDING OF THEIR NEEDS/INTENT (Chapters 7 & 8) and have established a TIME FOR YOUR MEETING. With all this information in order, you are ready to present your proposal. The next chapter explains in detail how to pull this information together in a Pivot-Point Presentation.

POINTS TO REMEMBER-
1. WANTS ARE EXPRESSIONS OF WAYS TO MEET NEEDS
2. USE THE OUTFRAME METHOD TO SHIFT LOGICAL LEVELS TO UNCOVER THE INTENT BEHIND SPECIFICATIONS THAT CONTAIN DEEPLY HIDDEN NEEDS
3. USE YOUR BACKTRACKING AND CONDITIONAL CLOSE SKILLS ALONG WITH THE CUSTOMER'S CRITERIA WORDS TO COME TO AGREEMENT ON THEIR NEEDS AND INTENT
4. KEEP A LIST OF ALL OF THE CLIENT"S CRITERIA WORDS AND PHRASES THAT YOU DISCOVER. USE THESE WORDS WHEN TRANSLATING SPECIFICATIONS INTO NEEDS AND INTENT

Chapter 9: Part 1

Now that you:
- Have your prospect's Criteria Words
- Know their Procedure for Buying Your Products or Service
- Have a Clear Understanding of their Needs / Intent
- Have Established a Time for Your Meeting

You are ready to present your proposal.

> **"Most speakers feel that 50 percent is what you deliver and 50 percent how you deliver it. Masters and Johnson feel the same way."**
> -Robed Orben

The first part of Step 5 in the **Green Light Selling** model is the Pivot-Point Presentation. This is the process where the needs of your prospect get associated (connected) to the features of your product or service. When the **Pivot-Point Presentation** is done properly, your product or service is bonded to the customer's need. When this bonding takes place, an ANCHOR is established.

ANCHORING

Anchoring is associating one idea or thing with another idea or thing. This association is an ongoing process and is also basically how people learn. You are creating ANCHORS for yourself and with others all the time but the process is going on unconsciously. That is, it is out of your normal day-to-day awareness. For example, most people have had the experience of hearing a word, or a song, or perhaps smelling something that instantly whisks them back to a past experience. For a brief moment, they vividly re-experience the event as though it was really happening again. The word, song, touch, etc. that triggered this vivid memory is an ANCHOR. The original experience is associated (bonded) to the ANCHOR (song, word, etc.).

When you interact with others, it is impossible to not create ANCHORS. The process usually occurs without you being consciously aware of it. Commercials and advertisements use ANCHORING to influence you to purchase specific products. Companies hope that by repeating their advertisement in a way that engages your emotions, you will think of their product (a specification) when you have a want or need to buy.

88

Anchoring In Action
To demonstrate the power of anchoring, think of Wheaties. Did your mind automatically remember the words, *"Breakfast of Champions?"* Which soft drink do you think of when you hear *"the real thing?"* This anchoring process does not in any way constrict your freedom of choice. You can still choose whether or not to buy any particular product. The association of Wheaties and *The Breakfast of Champions* that anchored in your brain creates the possibility that you will think of Wheaties when you think of cereal, or Coke when you are thirsty, and perhaps purchase those items to fill your immediate needs.

> **"Advertising created in the customer an insatiable desire for goods, and the installment plan gave him the immediate means to satisfy his desires."**
> -Henry Morton Robinson

WHAT THE PIVOT-POINT PRESENTATION DOES
One way to think of **PIVOT-POINT PRESENTATION** is to think of a door on a hinge. As the door is opened and closed, the hinge (although unmoving in it self) provides contact between the door and the doorway. In the same way, as you give your presentation, the prospect's criteria words allow contact between the needs of the customer and the solutions offered by the salesman. The pivot-points (CRITERIA WORDS) are how your customer represents their deep NEEDS to themselves.

- **The Pivot-Point Presentation anchors the customer's needs to your product or service.**

<u>Anchoring "Needs" To "Features"</u> Imagine your presentation is like the game of archery and your product features are displayed on pop-up targets. Each product feature has a separate target. If you have five features, there will be five different targets. The object is to shoot as many arrows as you can into each target (product feature) and strive to hit the bulls eye. The arrows are your criteria words. (See Figure 2-a.)
The bull's eye is the first feature of your product that you want to talk about. Your arrows -your prospect's criteria words - are propelled into the target. Some will miss, but most will strike the target and some will hit the bull's eye. Hitting the target bonds the

criteria word(s) and the feature together.

When you hit the bull's eye, you have satisfied the prospect's need with your product using his criteria words (Pivot Points). When you have connected as many criteria arrows as possible to the first feature, the target drops away and you are finished with it and will not shoot arrows at it again.

Then, your second feature target pops up. (See Figure 2-b.) You will shoot as many criteria arrows as possible into the second feature target (anchoring criteria arrows to this feature). When you have finished shooting as many criteria arrows as are reasonable, the second target drops away and feature target number three pops up, then four and five, etc. With each feature (target) you repeat this process.

Just like in archery, the first shots in your Pivot-Point Presentation may be way off the bull's eye or miss the board, but with practice you will become better. Soon, all your criteria arrows will be right on target. Using the Pivot-Point Presentation allows you to zero in on your sales goals with accuracy.

The criteria words (and phrases) that you discovered while establishing the prospects **NEEDS** and **INTENT** are used as the contact, or pivot point, of your selling presentation. It is important that during the sales process you are continually focused toward the fulfillment of those **NEEDS.**

THE THREE STEPS OF THE PIVOT-POINT PRESENTATION

1. **LISTEN** to your prospect's statement of need.
2. **BACKTRACK** (with elbow room as appropriate and *shift logical levels* when necessary) until you can state all of your prospect's *needs* in words (pivot points) that are consistent with his feelings and offer an adequate solution with the features of your product or service.
3. **OFFER YOUR PROPOSAL** by demonstrating how each feature and/or benefit of your product or service is related (offers a solution) to one or more of your prospect's needs (pivot points).

- **The Pivot-point Rule is : Every feature or benefit must be related to at least one pivot point (criteria word).**

Example
   1. LISTEN

   PROSPECT: "I want a three bedroom, 2,500 square foot, ranch-style home in the suburbs, not more than 20 minutes from my work, and I don't want to spend more than $125,000."

   2. BACKTRACK SALESMAN: "So, if I understand you correctly, you want a roomy, modem home that is convenient to your work place and fits your budget?"

   PROSPECT: "That's right.

Because the prospect verified the above backtrack as an adequate restatement of his needs the pivot points are:
   3. Roomy (substitutes for three bedrooms and 2,500 square foot home)
   4. Modem (substitutes for ranch-style and suburbs)
   5. Convenient to workplace (substitutes for 20 minutes from work)
   6. Fits your budget (substitutes for $125,000)

3. OFFER YOUR PROPOSAL

As you present your proposal, you must relate the features or benefits of your product or service to at least one pivot point (criteria word or phrase), similar to the ones below. *It is not permissible to say, "We have a house with a two-car garage, large yard, vaulted ceilings, family room, and near the bus lines that costs $125, 000."* This is simply a list of features that you have available. They have not been linked to any pivot points.

You could say, "Mr. Prospect, just this week we

listed a modern home in the Lake Park area, which is convenient to your work place. It is roomy even though it has two bedrooms, and it would fit your budget. If it were roomy enough and had that modern style, would you be interested in seeing this two bedroom home?"

REPARING FOR THE PRESENTATION

If your prospect is agreeable to seeing the house, you can then work up your Pivot-Point Presentation. To make your presentation easier, you can make a chart like the one below. Your chart will have two columns of information listing the features of the home and the associated pivot points.

Features of Home	Pivot-Points
1. Near bus lines	1. Roomy
2. costs $135,000	2. Modern
3. high vaulted ceiling in dinning room	3. convenient to work place
4. large family room	4. fits budget
5. kitchen recently remodeled garbage disposal & dishwasher installed	

Next, you decide in what way each feature relates to one or more of your prospect's **needs**. As you "present your story," you relate each **feature or benefit** of your product or service to as many of your prospect's needs as possible. Once you have related that feature to the appropriate need(s), you are finished presenting that feature. It is only mentioned again in closing. *Remember to shoot as many criteria arrows into each target (feature) as you can.*

Features of Home	Pivot-Points
1. NEAR BUS LINES	1. Roomy
2. costs $135,000	2. Modern
3. high vaulted ceiling in dinning room	**3. CONVENIENT TO WORK PLACE**
4. large family room	4. fits budget
5. kitchen recently remodeled garbage disposal & dishwasher installed	

The feature, **near the bus lines,** is related to the pivot- point 3, **convenient to work place**. You can describe this feature to your client in the following way. "You will find that this home is convenient to your workplace because it's near the bus lines."

Features of Home	Pivot-Points
1. Near bus lines	1. Roomy
2. COSTS $135,000	2. Modern
3. high vaulted ceiling in dinning room	3. Convenient to work place
4. large family room	**4. FITS BUDGET**
5. kitchen recently remodeled garbage disposal & dishwasher installed	

The second feature, **costs $135,000,** is related to pivot- point 4, **fits budget**. You can describe this feature to your client in the following way. "The fact that this place costs $135,000 means it fits your budget nicely." (You may have to demonstrate that this is a true fact. You could do this by comparing their annual income to the figure that most banks consider to be appropriate in terms of percentage of housing cost to annual income.)

Features of Home	Pivot-Points
1. Near bus lines	1. ROOMY
2. Costs $135,000	2. MODERN
3. HIGH VAULTED CEILING IN DINNING ROOM	3. Convenient to work place
4. large family room	4. Fits budget
5. kitchen recently remodeled garbage disposal & dishwasher installed	

The third feature, **high vaulted ceiling in dining room**, is related to pivot-points **1. roomy, and 2. modern.** The feature can be described to your client in the following way. "The high vaulted ceilings makes it feel roomy and offers a very modern appearance."

Features of Home	Pivot-Points
1. Near bus lines	1. ROOMY
2. Costs $135,000	2. MODERN
3. high vaulted ceiling in dinning room	3. Convenient to work place
4. LARGE FAMILY ROOM	4. Fits budget
5. kitchen recently remodeled garbage disposal & dishwasher installed	

The fourth feature, **large family room,** is related to pivot-points **1. roomy, and 2. modern.** The feature could be described to your client in the following way. "The large family room is roomy enough for any activity and has modern looking wallpaper."

Features of Home	Pivot-Points
1. Near bus lines	1. ROOMY
2. Costs $135,000	2. MODERN
3. high vaulted ceiling in dinning room	3. Convenient to work place
4. large family room	4. Fits budget
5. KITCHEN RECENTLY REMODELED- GARBAGE DISPOSAL & DISHWASHER INSTALLED	

The fifth feature, **kitchen recently remodeled - garbage disposal & dishwasher installed,** relates to pivot- points **1. roomy, and 2. modern.** The feature can be described to your client in the following way. "The kitchen was recently remodeled to make it more roomy and has all the modern conveniences, including the garbage disposal and dishwasher."

It is possible to have a large degree of latitude in using your pivot-points. As you go through the house, you can use the words on the right under pivot-points as many times as you wish to describe each additional feature of the home.

- **When using your PIVOT-POINTS lead with the FEATURE and connect the NEED.**

For example, when you meet with your prospect to show the house, you could say, "Notice the effect of this high vaulted ceiling and roomy feeling it gives. And right off the dining room is this large family room which is roomy enough to conveniently hold a hide-a-bed. Right over here is the kitchen, which was recently remodeled to make it more modern. The dishwasher was built in at that time. The garbage disposal, installed then also, is one of the most modern systems available. Right out the window you can see where the bus line connects, which makes it convenient to your work place. I'm confident you will agree that the cost, $76,000, fits your budget."

WHAT TO DO IF YOU MISINTERPRET A NEED

As you relate the features of your offering to your prospect's needs, they will not accept everything you say. They may correct you verbally or let you know with a non-verbal cue (such as a confused look or shaking their head "no") that you have guessed incorrectly about their underlying needs. If this should happen it is important that you stay in control of the situation. To stay in control:

- STOP whatever you are doing or saying. Continuing to pursue the current course usually only makes matters worse.
- ADMIT your mistake. This is a great time to let your prospects know that you need their help if you are going to be able to assist them in finding excellent solutions.
- IMMEDIATELY return to an area of agreement. Check your frames of rapport, safety zone (SZ), personal responsiveness (PR), and leveraged outcome (LO), by going back to some earlier part of the interaction where you were in agreement. This allows both of you a chance to recover your composure.
- WORK on some other issue before returning to the one that was a problem. Moving to another topic often brings out additional information that is useful and

assists in the resolution of the troublesome issue.

ACTION ITEM

"Major decisions usually require predictions about the future."
-Harry A. Builis

There are times during the selling process when it is beneficial to create an action item. With this process, you have your customer imagine "As If" they already have your product or service. This process gives them the experience of enjoying the benefits of the product or service, risk free. Projecting into the future is something people do naturally, when they think things such as, "I wonder what it would be like to have that new car." or "What would it be like if I were able to think of the appropriate words at the proper time?"

An Action Item Initiates Thoughts Of The Future
"As If ' It Were Now

For example, if you were selling computers, at some time in the presentation you could say:

> *"'Think about it this way. Currently you walk into your office in the morning and see papers all over the place and hear the noise of typewriters, which gives a feeling of disorder. If a customer calls up and says, 'I've got to get a loan today. How fast can you get me a financial statement?' the whole office is thrown into an uproar.*
>
> *Now, suppose it is a year from now. The system is in and everyone is accustomed to it. When you walk into your office you notice the absence of paper clutter. It is quiet, with a*

feeling of efficiency. If a customer calls up and wants a financial statement that day you can easily say, "No problem. We can have it by one o'clock." You can tell your bookkeepers what you need, they push a few buttons and then quickly hand you the financial statement you need.

One way to create an action item is ask, "What would it be like... ?'" or "Think of a time in the future when..." or "Pretend you already have... " You will probably discover that most people are already doing this to some degree and need only a little encouragement to initiate the process.

We kept our example of selling a home using PIVOT- POINT PRESENTATION simple and straightforward. We now return to Boyd, where we give a more involved example of Pivot-Point Presentation.

Chapter 9:Part 2

THE MODEL IN ACTION
Preparing for the Presentation

When we left Boyd, he had just made an appointment to meet Don. Before they met, Don compiled a chart listing Boyd's needs and some of the features of the training. He will give his proposal, using Boyd's criteria words, unwind, make money, reduce the stress, confident glow, valuable, fun, and challenge.

Features of Training	Pivot-Points
1. How to enter new market profitably	1. Make more money
2. How to close 75% to 85% of sales	2. Reduce stress
3. How to identify a person's convincer strategy	3. Become a top notch salesman a. develop abilities b. gain confidence c. retain composure d. keep control of the selling process
4. What "Power Words" are and how they work	
5. How to analyze your own best motivational strategy	

It's Time To Meet Boyd In Person

[Note: Features are in italic, Pivot Points in Bold Face]

DON: "Thank you for coming in today, Boyd. Just to make certain that we make good use of your valuable use of your time, let me review for just a moment what you want from a sales training. Now, if I understand correctly, you want to become a **top notch salesman** so that you can make more money and **reduce the stress** of your work."

BOYD: "That's correct."

[Feature 1. How to enter new markets profitably.]

DON: "One of the features of our sales training will help you to **develop your abilities** in such a way that it will allow you to *enter new sales markets profitably*, and gain **confidence** in a way that will greatly **reduce the stress** you would ordinarily feel. You may find that as you meet the challenge of *entering a new area for selling*, you will develop that confident glow, allowing you to **keep control of the selling process** in a way that will cause you to **make more money.** You may even notice there is a degree of fun in *entering a new market,* as you find yourself able to retain composure as you become a top notch salesman." (Feature 1 was related to all 7 pivot points!)

> (The above dialogue may sound to you as if it would not make sense to the prospect. It has been our experience that when you use the client's pivot points (the client's criteria words and phrases) and relate them to the features of your product or service, your customer will understand what you are saying. This is because they will translate the criteria words into whatever personal meaning that they have previously associated to the words. You gain more confidence in using these rather unusual sentences after you have worked with them for a while.)

[Feature 2. How to close 75% to 85% of sales.]

"As you further **gain confidence** in your newly **developed abilities,** we will show you valuable techniques that will promote a *75 % to 85 % closure of your sales,* which will, of course, **make you more money and reduce stress**. As you learn new ways to **control the selling process**, you may be surprised at how fun it is to meet the challenge of **becoming a top notch salesman.**" (Feature 2 was related to 6 pivot points.)

[Feature3. How to identify a person's convincer strategy.]

"One of the techniques that will help you make **more money** is how to *identify a person's convincer strategy.* You may find that learning how people make decisions will **develop your abilities** in a way that will greatly **reduce stress**, allowing you to **retain your composure** in the kinds of situations that even a **top notch salesman** may find himself in from time to time. And even those kinds of situations are valuable in that they allow you to **gain confidence** in how to **keep control of the selling situation.**" (Feature 3 related to 7 pivot points.)

[Feature 4. What Power Words are and how they work.]

"We have found that one of the things that is most valuable in helping a salesman **gain confidence** in his abilities and **retain his composure** is to have a full understanding of *"Power Words' and how they work.* Being at ease with language is valuable in that it helps **reduce stress** to the point that he is able to **keep control of the selling process,** wearing that confident glow the way only a **top notch salesman** can. *Learning about "Power Words"* will help you *make more money.* " (Feature 4 related to 6 pivot points.)

[Feature 5. How to analyze your own best motivational strategy.]

"Another feature that is extremely valuable for any **top notch salesman** to possess is the ability to *analyze his own best motivational strategy.* What is it that causes you to get out of bed in the morning with that confident glow, eager to face the challenge of making more money? What is it that motivates you to **develop abilities** in a way that **reduces stress as you gain confidence** in your ability to **keep control of the selling process**? We help you to answer these and many more questions during this sales training." (Feature 5 relates to 5 pivot-points.)

When you give your presentation, each feature is related to each of the prospect's needs showing them how the features or benefits can be a way for them to attain what they want. It is important to keep your voice tone friendly, never pushy, demonstrating that you respect your prospect's free choice.

OTHER FACTORS TO CONSIDER
When you discovered the steps to your prospect's buying procedures, you discovered how to set up green lights for this sale. When they verbalized those steps, they also gave you a form of commitment. At the same time, the prospect(s) preconditioned their minds to the flow of the future selling process. They agreed that if you were able to

satisfy all the requirements of the first step of their buying procedure, they would move to the second step. If you were able to meet all of the requirements for steps one and two, they would move to step three, and so on through to the end.

As they made those commitments moving from one step to the next, in their minds it was almost as if the first condition had already been satisfied, before they moved to the second. It really was not and must still be satisfied during your presentation. They will give you the benefit of the doubt.

When you finally make your presentation and move toward closing the sale, you encounter the steps in their buying procedure that have not actually been resolved. The client will have a tendency to help you satisfy these steps by giving you the information and assistance you need. They want you to succeed, and will help you move through the green lights. From this point in the **Green Light Selling** model we move to the close.

POINTS TO REMEMBER-

1. ANCHORING CREATES THE NECESSARY ASSOCIATION BETWEEN THE CUSTOMER'S NEED AND YOUR PRODUCT
2. YOUR CUSTOMER'S NEEDS / CRITERIA WORDS ARE PIVOT POINTS
3. THE FEATURES AND BENEFITS OF YOUR PRODUCT MUST BE RELATED TO PIVOT POINTS
4. PREPARE YOUR PRESENTATION LISTING FEATURES & PIVOT POINTS IN COLUMNS
5. MATCHING THE FEATURES OF YOUR PRODUCT WITH THE PIVOT POINTS, ANCHORS THE PRODUCT IN THEIR MIND
6. CREATE AN ACTION ITEM TO GIVE YOUR CLIENT THE EXPERIENCE OF HAVING YOUR PRODUCT / SERVICE NOW
7. IF YOU HAVE MISINTERPRETED A NEED
   - Stop
   - Admit your mistake
   - Return to an area of agreement
   - Work on some other issue before returning to the problem issue

Chapter 10

"The decision is maybe and that's final."
-Anonymous

Have you ever noticed how once you get the idea to buy something, it has a tendency to stay on your mind until you buy it? Perhaps you have had the experience of becoming mildly dissatisfied with your car. Your interest in new cars grew and grew until you finally took action and closed the issue by buying a new vehicle.

In similar fashion, your **prospects want to have their needs met.** Once they have come to the point of dissatisfaction with their current state of affairs, and you have demonstrated that you have real solutions (setting the green lights in place), **they want closure.** They want you to carry them with you and complete the sales process. If you handle them properly, your customer will even help you paddle the boat and stay on course. After you have given your presentation and related all the features of your product or service to each of your prospect's needs, you are ready for the close.

- **Don't introduce "new information" at the close, you will only confuse everyone including yourself.**

When you reach the close, you must keep your information based primarily on what's already been covered. This speeds up the closure process and can enable you to close large sales in one session. Introducing new information at the close confuses your customer and delays the sale. Customers find it hard to evaluate any new information at this juncture. Adding extra information at the close will most likely delay their "yes" response and result in annoying callbacks.

DISCOVERING YOUR CLIENT'S CONVINCER STRATEGY

"You never know what is enough unless you know what is more than enough.
-William Blake

Your prospects must be convinced that your product or service matches their needs before you can successfully close the order. Each person has an internal process that they go through before they believe a product or service is right for them. It is almost as if people have "internal barometers," and that they have to reach some threshold before they can have the experience of feeling "I AM CONVINCED." People fill their barometers with what they see or hear or feel about a product until they reach the point that says, 'Enough, I believe you now.' (See Figures 3a and 3b.) *While people are the same in that they all have internal barometers, each individual has a different process they go through to get to their ENOUGH POINT.* **How they fill it** *to the enough point (where they are convinced)* **has a direct relationship to their buying strategy.**

Filling the Internal Barometer

Your internal barometer is filled when you process input from your senses (mainly visual, auditory, and kinesthetic) and draw on your remembered information and your past experiences for reference.

While some people have a preference for seeing (visual) evidence that something is true, others prefer hearing (auditory) about products or services. Another group of individuals require doing something (kinesthetic) before they are totally convinced. Time can also be a factor. At one end of the scale are those people who only need to hear or see something only one time. At the other end of the scale, there are people who are never totally convinced. The majority of people are in the middle of the continuum somewhere. Most people require seeing or hearing evidence about your product two to three times before they become convinced. Some people are only convinced after they "take part in a physical demonstration" to test the product for themselves.

> **"I am the world's worst salesman: therefore I must make it easy for people to buy.**
> -F. W. Woolworth

All "normal" people have some way of reaching a decision. Even individuals who are never totally convinced have some way of eventually deciding to buy. Here are two questions you can ask people to discover their convincer strategy. Question 1 tells you the sensory method your prospects use to evaluate evidence. Question 2 tells you how many times the client will require you to supply evidence before they are likely to make a decision.

Question 1

1. **"How do you know that someone else is good at what they do?"**

(Their answers will fall into one of these categories.)

a. **See** it. (Your client prefers to see evidence.)

b. **Hear** about it. (Your client prefers to hear evidence.)

c. **Do it** with them. (Your client prefers a physical demonstration or test period.)

d. **Read** about it. (Your client prefers to read brochures, reviews, testimonials, charts, and graphs.)

Then ... Question 2

2. How often does someone have to demonstrate competency to you before you are convinced?"

a. An **AUTOMATIC** can either say, "One time" or "I assume they do a good job unless the person shows me otherwise." This person is easy to sell.

b. A **CONSISTENT** will probably say, "Each time." This person is often hard to sell because they are never convinced. For them it usually requires special language to close the sale.

c. A **NUMBER OF TIMES** person will give you a figure for an answer. This person usually wants to see and or hear about the product or service 2 or 3 times.

d. The last category is **A PERIOD OF TIME** person. For these people, a specific length of time has to have elapsed -days, weeks, or months. In order to sell them, you may have to allow them to use the product or service for the specified length of time.

You must be aware that each person has their own particular combination of answers to Questions 1 and 2. That means you must be as flexible as possible in offering your evidence. Be prepared to go over the same information several times if necessary. People who need to see convincing evidence 2 or 3 times **do not necessarily need different evidence each time.** Often all you need to do to close the sale is to do a thorough recap of your previous presentation. In fact, if you have a sales opportunity right now that has been "hanging fire" for a long time, just try going back in and giving your entire presentation one more time. You might be pleasantly surprised to find that this is all that is needed to bring the prospect to closure.

CHOOSING LANGUAGE FOR THE CLOSE

Sorting Styles

People SORT (or filter into their awareness) and use only the parts of a conversation that is meaningful to them and that they can understand. For example, a person who is color blind would discard most of what another person says as they describe a "really colorful scene." The way they SORT for meaning would reject the talk of colorful things. In general, people have specific SORTING STYLES that they use to filter what is useful information or not.

You can find the right words to convince your client if you know how the client sorts for information. The Language and Behavior Profile by Rodger Bailey outlines in detail ways to detect how your prospect sorts for information to motivate themselves into action. Some of the sorting principles are briefly mentioned here. These are not hard and fast categories. Again, most people fall somewhere in-between the two types given. Determine how your client fits into the profile below. By directing your language so that you accommodate how they motivate themselves, you obtain optimum results.

General / Specific

The **GENERAL** person thinks in terms of the big picture. Although they recognize details, they have difficulty focusing on specifics. Most of the time, these individuals talk without modifiers and proper nouns and their focus is random. For the **GENERAL** person, you use words that give the overall picture like, "Your type of business requires good management and prudent marketing."

The **SPECIFIC** person likes more detail and only understands things when they are given details in sequence. These individuals use proper nouns to describe persons and places. Phrases like, "This training will provide you with ways to motivate your employees in their duties of filling and delivering orders... " catch the attention of the **SPECIFIC**.

Proactive / Reactive

PROACTIVE persons are action oriented. They love to be in a position to motivate and initiate projects. They may think about their actions after the fact. These individuals talk with authority and refer to the projects in the active or completed tense. **PROACTIVES** respond positively to "do it," "make it happen," and "go for it."

The **REACTIVE** person loves to analyze the situation. Being cautious, they seek out situations where they can understand or think about options. These individuals tend to use long sentences with passive verbs. **REACTIVES** prefer ideas presented to them with cautious words such as, "wait," "get prepared," and "take advantage of the best opportunity that comes along."

Away From / Toward

The **AWAY FROM** individual buys a product if it prevents them from a situation they want to avoid. **AWAY FROMS** are always looking for problems in the smallest of situations. Not particularly goal oriented, these individuals talk about eliminating or missing things. They are often looked upon as negative. For the **AWAY FROM** person, you can use phrases like "Our product allows you to avoid the problem of..." or "Our service prevents this from happening."

The **TOWARDS** person is out to gain from their encounters. Words like "Include,' "having," and "attain," are a major part of their vocabulary. These individuals are happiest when working toward a goal. The **TOWARDS** person is motivated with phrases like, "As you move toward the goal you have set for yourself" or "Looking ahead to where your company can be."

Internal / External

The **INTERNAL** needs to decide and evaluate information on their own. Self motivated, these individuals feel they are the only ones that can even evaluate themselves. Their opinions would probably begins with the words "I know." It is important to use words such as "You know within your self" or "You need to decide for yourself" with **INTERNAL** people.

The **EXTERNAL** wants others to decide for him. These individuals accept information from others as fact. They follow the leaders (buy when others buy) and are most comfortable with checklists, references, and standards. **EXTERNALS** respond well to phrases like, "I can tell you, and others can assure you" or "Our testimonials are evidence to you.

If you do not know which category type your prospect falls into, you can use both types of language simultaneously. People tend to listen to words that match their internal sorting processes and delete the rest of the information that doesn't fit their viewpoint. If you were to use a phrase such as, "You know within yourself, and others can assure you." the INTERNAL person would pick up on the first phrase, deleting the second, and the EXTERNAL person would pick up on the second phrase, deleting the first.

PUTTING YOUR PROSPECT IN A POSITION TO BUY

Physiology For A "YES" Decision

Did you realize that there are body postures that prevent people from being able to decide? For just a moment, pretend that you are being asked if you would like to buy an attractive article of clothing. Pretend that you really like it, you can afford it, and that you can justify the purchase.

Now slump down in your chair, cross your legs, squeeze most of the air out of your lungs, and tilt your head to one side. Holding that position, imagine the sales clerk asking if you want to buy the article of clothing. Notice how hard it is to feel convinced that this would be a good decision.

Now, sit up straight or stand up, lift your head high, and breathe comfortably. Again, holding that position imagine the sales clerk asking if you want to buy the article of clothing. Notice that this posture makes it easier to evaluate your internal barometer (Figure 3-a) and make a firm decision to make the purchase.

The optimal posture for making a *"yes decision"* is with the body in a symmetrical position. The centerline of the body must be straight. There has to be adequate oxygen in the lungs (don't ask the customer to buy if he has just run up a flight of stairs!), minimal tension in the shoulders, and the chin slightly tucked.

> **"Nothing is more difficult, and therefore more precious than to be able to decide.**
> -Napoleon Bonaparte

Make sure your prospect is in an optimal posture before you go into your closing sequence. One way of doing this is to be in the optimal posture yourself. If your rapport frames are intact, your prospect will probably follow your lead. If in doubt, do whatever is necessary to get the prospect up and moving around before you close. It's a shame to see a well-planned sales presentation come to a halt when the prospect is in a posture that cannot possible support a yes decision.

CONSTRUCTING YOUR CLOSING STATEMENT

From the very beginning, you have been following your prospect's procedure for buying. Although you have a special structure for your selling process (Rapport Frames,

Procedure Elicitation, Needs Elicitation, Get to Intent, Pivot-Point Presentation, and Close), you have used all these elements within your customer's buying procedure.

Up to this point, you have:
- Established a step-by-step list (in writing) of their procedure for buying.
- Found the prospect's outcome (what they need - what they want) and translated it into Pivot points.
- Constructed a representative list of criteria words that have a positive emotional impact on your prospect.

You use all three of these elements in constructing your closing statement.

You structure the closing statement with the prospect's step-by-step procedure for buying. Keep the customer's buying steps in the **exact** order that they gave them to you. Following their buying procedure sequence makes your close seem logical to them.

Building Your Recap

You then can interweave their pivot-points and criteria words into each step of their buying process as you recap your presentation to your customer. This addition of your customer's criteria words makes a high powered close.

After all, you are organizing all the prospect's data in a form that is logical and easy for them to understand. How can they possibly say no to information they gave you! Every-thing matches with the way they operate. There is nothing they can argue with.

Being aware of your client's convincer strategy and the methods that persuade them gives you ample information for your close. At first, the words and phrases you deliver may sound nonsensical to you, but the impact is powerful for your client. (See Boyd Buys 1 Closing the Sale later in this chapter for an example of a closing statement.)

LOOKING FOR YES

The Final Closing Statement

After you go through the step-by-step recap, you come to the final closing statement. If you've done a professional job and like to close (as opposed to having sales close themselves), this close works very well.

To use this close, you have to have all your ducks lined up. You have already found out the customer's OUTCOME (what they need - what they want). You have given your PROPOSAL. You have discussed the terms of time, money, commitments of one sort or another that you're going to have to make. You have already quoted them the price and indicated some general idea of how the money is to be paid. **Every step up to this point has to be covered. Otherwise this close won't work.** You can use this close on the one who pays the money or the one who is the decision maker.

The Formula

The formula is as follows:
1. You begin with the word **NOW.**
2. The next few words depend on the circumstance. You can select from the following choices that fit your situation (or make up a similar scenario that fits your needs). You then say:

    "WE GOT TOGETHER TODAY BECAUSE..."

    "WE ARE HERE TODAY BECAUSE..."

    "YOU CALLED THIS MEEETING TODAY BECAUSE..."

    "YOU CAME IN TODAY BECAUSE..."
3. The next phrase is:

    "YOU DECIDED TO DO SOMETHNG (insert their criteria word(s) here _____) ABOUT _____ .

And then you fill in the blank with the name of the problem as they understand it. Whatever is their understanding of the problem.

"your data systems requirements"

"your air pollution problem"

"your future financial needs"

"about your in service training requirement"

4. Then...

    **"SO, I WOULD LIKE TO
    _____ AS SOON AS
    POSSIBLE FOR ALL THE OBVIOUS
    REASONS."**

    You fill in the blank with what you want to do for them.
    "I would like to schedule the in-service training"

    "I would like to pick up your insurance policies"

    "I would like to get some X-rays"

    "I would like to show you the warehouse"

    "I would like to do a thorough testing of the air"
5. IS THIS WHAT YOU WOULD LIKE TO DO?
6. THEN YOU SHUT UP, and they say yes. Every single time.

Example of an effective closing statement:

"You've come in today because you've decided to do something permanent about your insurance needs. If this is what you'd like to do, I'd like to evaluate your policies as soon as possible for all the obvious reasons. Is this what you'd like to do?"

And then they say yes!

> **"When your work speaks for itself, don't interrupt."**
> -Henry J. Kaiser

THE MODEL IN ACTION

The close is where we again use the information we have gathered about Boyd's buying procedure, criteria words, and pivot points.

Boyd's Buying Procedure
1. CONSIDERED ALL THE IMPORTANT FACTORS
2. RETAINS FLEXIBILITY FOR ATTENDANCE
3. WORTH THE TIME INVESTED
4. COST CONSIDERATION MET
5. "DO IT"

Boyd's Criteria Words / Phrases

Boyd's list of criteria words and phrases includes fun, unwind, challenge, make more money, reduce the stress, confident glow, valuable, and flexibility. He said the word challenge twice. While he did not actually use the word flexible himself, he agreed with its use three times.

Boyd's Pivot-Points

1. Make more money
2. Reduce stress
3. Become a top notch salesman
   a. develop abilities
   b. gain confidence
   c. retain composure
   d. keep control of the selling process

"Nothing is more satisfying than when timing and delivery occur in perfect sequence."
-Anonymous

With this information in hand, you can now go into your close, using language similar to the following. To more easily see how the components come together, Boyd's procedure is CAPITALIZED, his **pivot points are bolded,** and his criteria words are italicized.

Boyd Buys - Closing The Sale

DON: "As you look at the list on this chart of the things we have discussed, you can see with a degree of **confidence** that we CONSIDERED ALL THE IMPORTANT FACTORS concerning techniques that will allow you to **develop abilities** in keeping with the performance of a **top notch salesman.** This schedule, listing the dates of the sales training, shows that because the trainings are held in several different locations at different times, YOU RETAIN COMPLETE FLEXIBILITY FOR ATTENDANCE, **reducing any stress** that might otherwise be connected with your decision, at the same time moving toward your goal of **becoming a top notch salesman.** In fact, it is perfectly allowable to attend the first session in one city and the second in a different, if your travel schedule so dictates. I think you will agree that the items we mentioned will build your ability to **retain your composure** as you consider that the many things covered in these sales training are *valuable* and WORTH THE TIME INVESTED. You know within yourself, and others can assure you, that **keeping control of the selling process** will allow you to have your COST CONSIDERATIONS met in a way that is *challenging and fun,* allowing you to close 75 % to 85 % of your sales."

"Boyd, you came in today because you want to do something about your desire to **reduce the stress** of being a top notch salesman by **making more money.** If this is what you'd like to do, I'd like to sign you up for this training as soon as possible, for all the obvious reasons. Is this what you want to do?"

At this point you close your mouth, watch for the non-verbal answer, and wait. Remember, *"yes"* is a head nod up and down, *"no"* is a shake back and forth, and *"I don't know"* is a shrug. If you watch for this non-verbal answer, you know before your prospects open their mouths whether they are going to say yes or no. If you can see that a prospect is hesitant, it may only mean that you have not adequately covered all the needs, or that there is perhaps an unspoken need (hidden agenda) that has not yet been covered.

POINTS TO REMEMBER
1. YOUR PROSPECT WANTS CLOSURE
2. EVERYONE HAS A DECISION STRATEGY
3. FIND HOW YOUR CLIENT SORTS FOR INFORMATION AND HOW MANY TIMES THEY NEED TO SEE EVIDENCE
4. BE WILLING TO PRESENT YOUR CONVINCING INFORMATION SEVERAL TIMES IF NECESSARY
5. DETERMINE HOW YOUR CLIENT SORTS AND PROJECT PHRASES THAT WILL MOTIVATE THEM
6. CONSTRUCT THE CLOSE BY GOING THROUGH THE PROSPECT"S BUYING STRATEGY, ADDING THEIR CRITERIA WORDS AND PIVOT POINTS
7. FOLLOW THE SIX STEPS TO CONSTRUCT YOUR FINAL CLOSING STATEMENT

Chapter 11

When you enter your prospect's life, your interactions (however brief or prolonged they may be) produce ripples of change. From the first moments of your INITIAL BENEFIT STATEMENT, the relationship you establish alters the client's perception of the world around them. Establishing the FRAMES OF RAPPORT and helping your prospects to clarify their OUTCOMES sets in motion processes that, if continued, will either be a hindrance or a benefit.

Preparing for your exit gives you the opportunity to take care of the final details so that when you exit, you are re-enforcing an ever enriching relationship. This is similar to finishing the building of a house. Storing the tools you used for your project does not mean you have to discard them. Closing the sale does not mean you end the relationship. You are exiting this stage of the relationship only to return again in the future to offer either service or a referral. There are three distinct stages to closing the sale. Structuring your exit around these three elements promotes the relationship you have been developing and produces a wealth of future business for your efforts.

EXPLORING FUTURE POSSIBILITIES

You want to make a favorable impact on the customer before exiting. A good impression will prompt your customer to remember your service and offer you repeat business. There are two ways that this can be done. The first is to encourage the client set up future appointments. This action is an indication of the client's intention of maintaining a continued relationship. Another possibility is for you to set up meetings with mutual acquaintances. These could be social meetings or meetings with other professionals that you come in contact with in your daily selling.

If you have several customers, it is very likely that they don't know each other, but that they may have common interests or complimentary services. For example, two of your clients may have resources that are mutually beneficial, but they may not know one another. Offer them the opportunity to meet one another. This, in turn, opens the door for your customers to tell you about their contacts. This is an indication of the client's commitment to developing more trust and deepening your relationship.

Discuss Future Needs

Encourage your client to talk about needs they anticipate in the future. Even if their future needs are just hopes and dreams right now, when they tell you about their possible future requirements, it indicates your interest in a continued relationship with them.

- **Show your customer that you have a genuine interest in their future.**

Probe for other needs, even if you can't satisfy them. Their needs may be outside the realm of your product or service, but even if you can't satisfy the requirements, you may be able to direct them to resources or competent people who can. Directing *your client to your contacts* helps strengthen your relationship with the customer and increases the level of trust.

SET PROCEDURES FOR HANDLING FUTURE PROBLEMS

You extend GREEN LIGHTS into the future by anticipating problems and providing solutions before they occur. Every time you anticipate a problem and learn what actions you need to provide to the customer for them to be satisfied, you will be ahead. You accomplish this by asking the client for possible problem scenarios that might arise, and then backtrack solutions. Asking them for information means you can be instrumental in providing solutions if problems do arise.

Elicit Customer's Procedure For Dealing With Problems and Backtrack

Backtrack all possible problems that you think could realistically occur. Simply ask your client, "If the following circumstances come up, what is your procedure for dealing with them?"

If, for example, you sell computer equipment, ask the client *"What is your procedure for protecting and storing data, or what sort of fall-back plans do you have in the event of a fire."* This provides you with an opportunity to offer alternate ways to assist the client in an emergency situation.

Assuming a worst-case scenario demonstrates to the prospect that you are on your toes and taking a professional interest in their needs by handling the details.

> **"Long-range planning does not deal with future decisions, but with the future of present decisions."**
> -Peter F. Drucker

Handling Details Strengthens Relationship

My real estate agent used this principle to help us purchase a home. After we made the offer on our home but before the contract was signed, she insisted that we pay $200 to have an outside engineer come in and do a complete inspection of the house. Her suggestion provided 3 effects. First of all, it let us know she was professional and looking out for our interests. (We wouldn't have thought of an inspection.) Secondly, our commitment to the sale was increased. When the favorable engineer's report came back, we were more committed because we had more money on the table. Finally, it sold us on the product. The results allowed us to have a better understanding of the product before we signed the papers. The sale went smoother because of this wise move on the realtor's part. Even if the engineer's report indicated a problem with the home, we would have grown even closer to that real estate agent for protecting our interests. This type of forethought emphasizes relationship and enhances the salesperson's professionalism in the eyes of the buyer.

Give Your Procedure For Responding to Problems

Let your customer know how you will respond to their problems. If you sell copier equipment, you would make statements like, *"This is the number that you call,"* *"Our company will respond to your request within 1 hour,"* or *" You will have a trained key operator."* After you let them know what your procedure for handling problems is, also verify that they understand.

Get Criteria for Successful Problem Resolution

Ask your client how they would know you had solved their problem successfully. Then backtrack and do a conditional close. Suppose that your client's electric stapler goes down at the worst possible moment... how would they judge whether your response was adequate? Would getting the advertising packets out 24-hours late be satisfactory? Would bringing in replacement equipment or sending out the rest of their project to another jobber be equally satisfactory for them? Ask for specifics. Asking up front about future problems lets the client know that they will be assisted to their satisfaction.

- **It is better to know what their criteria are now than when they are actually having a problem.**

Every time you project your customer into a theoretical problem that they imagine, and then bring them back out, you are building a green light sequence. In effect, you are preprocessing barriers that could come between you and the client. Most salespeople want to speed through the EXIT when the thought of future problems and servicing come up. Before you sign the contract, take the opportunity to handle the future. Working out problems prior to signing the contract deepens your existing relationship.

SIGNING THE CONTRACT

Go Over Contract In Detail

To insure that your prospect understands the agreement, go over the contract in extreme detail. Recap each of the elements of your contract no matter how long it is. It is not a good idea to let them sign a contract without reading and understanding the terms. This heads off last minute objections.

Signatures

It is best if your contract requires two signatures. The salesperson and the customer should both have a place to sign. If your contracts are not set up this way, it's worth talking to your management about changing the format of your standard contract. Contracts that only allow for the customer to sign and then get sent to your home office are asymmetrical. The element of symmetry makes the client feel more equal and at ease with you.

Quickly Review Your Next Appointment

After you sign the contract, set up a future contact date. This creates a new picture in your client's mind beyond today's sale and toward your next opportunity to work together.

Leave

I have a dear friend who tells me "goodbye" four times before she leaves. While socially this may be acceptable, in a business situation people are not as tolerant of prolonged good-byes. When the sale is closed, it is time to exit.

After you have signed and set up a future appointment, leave. Don't hang around unless you have something else to accomplish. If you do not leave at this time, the customer will slowly begin to slide into buyer's remorse. It doesn't have to do with you or them, that's just the way it happens; it's a psychological issue. The customer will begin to bring up other objections and issues and you won't have adequate answers.

Send Written Note

Send your customer a personal note or letter within 24 hours thanking them for the order. Make the note simple and brief (1-2 paragraphs). Your note doesn't have to be anything more than thanks a lot, I'm looking forward to visiting you on our next appointment. A handwritten note is nice if it is appropriate to your product and your position in the business.

Your client will look at your note and get a warm fuzzy feeling. This ingredient helps combat buyer's remorse. By the time you visit your client again, everything will be fine. When the time comes, you will be ready to begin the process all over again with the Entrance.

POINTS TO REMEMBER

1. DISCUSS FUTURE NEEDS WITH YOUR CLIENT TO INDICATE INTEREST IN RELATIONSHIP
2. SET PROCEDURES FOR HANDLING PROBLEMS
3. ELICIT CUSTOMER'S PROCEDURE FOR DEALING WITH PROBLEMS AND BACKTRACK
4. GIVE YOUR PROCEDURE FOR RESPONDING TO PROBLEMS
5. GET CRITERIA FOR SUCCESSFUL PROBLEM RESOLUTION
6. INSURING PROBLEM RESOLUTION DEEPENS RELATIONSHIP
7. GO OVER CONTRACT IN DETAIL TO INSURE UNDERSTANDING
8. HAVE A CONTRACT THAT ALLOWS BOTH SALESPERSON AND CLIENT TO SIGN
9. WHEN YOU ARE DONE - LEAVE
10. SEND A WRITTEN PERSONAL NOTE OR LETTER WITHIN 24 HOURS THANKING THE CLIENT FOR THE ORDER

Chapter 12

There is more to **Green Light Selling** than just learning the steps you go through to sell your client. The other major ingredient is you. The way your project yourself to your clientele is very important. Equally important is targeting the market you want to sell to and defining exactly who is in that market. Doing this preliminary work makes your **Green Light Selling** much more effective.

ATTITUDES FOR EFFECTIVE SELLING

Your attitude speaks louder than words. The attitude you project to your customer speaks volumes about how you will treat them. If your attitude leads the customer to believe that you are not there for their best interest, you may as well walk away. While cultivating valuable business relationships, learn to maintain an attitude that compliments your customer. There are three attitudes (presuppositions) that you need to maintain during the selling process. Those three attitudes are:

- **Behind every behavior is a positive intention.**
- **People are always behaving the best they can with the understanding they have at the time.**
- **The meaning of the communication is the response it generates in other people.**

To effectively use the **Green Light Selling** model, you need to make sure your attitude supports these ideas. The material covered in this book is not as effective if you do not implement these three ideas into your daily thinking. Watch your reactions to your customer's words and actions. Adjusting your knee-jerk reactions to what customers do and say, and filtering your reaction through these three attitudes helps you be more professional and successful.

- **Remember, the only time it makes any difference whatsoever that you believe these ideas, is in those moments when you don't.**

Behind Every Behavior Is A Positive Intention

This means that it is best to assume that your customer always has a positive intention. Your brain has the ability to separate out the client's behavior from the client's intention behind the behavior ... no matter how devastating, nasty, or rotten a behavior might be. People tend to physically act out or verbally lash out in order to protect themselves, defend others, or hide important information they don't want you to have access to.

For example, your customer may be doing everything in their power to suggest that you leave. Your interpretation of the situation is that they are no longer interested in your product. Your knee-jerk reaction might be to press on and continue to show your product so they will consider it.

> **"No customer can be worse than 'no' customer."**
> -Leopold Fechtner

What you don't know is that the individual you are presenting your product to may have a 2:30 appointment with their boss or a 3:00 appointment with their eye doctor. Your customer may be so excited about your product that they want to call a special meeting in order to authorize funds for purchase. Assuming that "YOU KNOW" what their intention is may be detrimental to your welfare and could ultimately hurt the outcome of your sale. The wrong attitude puts you in a defensive mode and your client may think you are hostile or ambivalent.

So, when you find yourself saying.-

- **"They just have a negative intention,"**
- **"They're just indecisive,"**
- **"They're just doing that to make me mad,"**
- **"He knows better than that, " or**
- **"They're just wasting my time by putting me off. "**

Stop your mile-a-minute brain and say, "Wait a minute, POSITIVE INTENT. I know they have a positive intention." Your brain will still tell you "No it isn't. Not this one. This is the exception." And it is at that moment you really need to take control of yourself!

People Are Always Behaving The Best They Can With The Understanding They Have At The Time.

While interacting with your client, remember they are always selecting the best behavior from their menu of choices that they have available at the moment. If you do not maintain an attitude that supports this idea, again you presume a negative intention. You may catch yourself thinking things such as:

- "They thought of the right thing to do and then didn't do it."
- "I know why they did that, just to jerk my chain and rattle my cage and give me a bad time."
- "They wanted to ruin my day."
- "People like them always do that kind of stuff because they're indecisive."

During moments of stress while you are selling, know that the client is behaving in the best way that they have available to them at the time. If you rely on your pre-wired "those indecisive jerks" response, your sales techniques break down. Your client will go along with you for the moment but, in the end they won't go through with the deal. They'll eventually find a reason to get out of the situation and your **Green Light Selling** techniques are useless.

The Meaning Of The Communication Is The Response It Generates In Other People.

Have you ever had a customer who just didn't understand you? As you explained your statement over and over, THEY just didn't seem to get it! Most people think, "My communication means what I say it means, what I think it means; and if you respond in a weird way, it's because I haven't said it loud enough or often enough." Continuing to say and do the same thing(s) over and over is actually useless. What usually happens is the response doesn't change and so the sender of the communication believes the **receiver** is either stupid or that they have an attitude problem. In many communications these are the only two possibilities the participants see.

Well, that's not the way it should be. The attitude you need to acquire is that the meaning of the communication is described and defined by the responder NOT by the one sending the communication. That means **your client's** response indicates the result of what you have said.

First, recognize if your client is responding to or interpreting your communication the wrong way. If they are, then imagine what kind of positive intention this person could have *based on the response they are giving you.* Then, you can change your behavior to accommodate your new understanding and to get a different response. How they respond in turn (what they do) tells you what the meaning of your communication was to them. Continue to adjust your communication until the response you want is received.

In the following conversation, Bud is receiving constructive criticism from Tom.

> Tom: "I have some constructive criticism for you on your letter."

> Bud: "Tom, if you don't like my work, don't read it."

> Tom: "No, that wasn't my intention. I think this is great work and I really think it would get your point across if you changed this one little piece in the sentence. And you know, I think it's a wonderful letter."

> Bud: (Sarcastically) "Yeah, right."

Bud has defined what Tom's communication means. He thinks Tom doesn't like his work. Bud didn't hear the part of Tom's communication that said "I like it." If Tom realizes that his communication was not received the way he had intended, he might quickly take another tact. For example, he might suggest they talk while taking a walk or some other pleasant distraction. Then he could use different words to explain to Bud (Because he's the one who decides what Tom's communication means.)

Having the attitude that the response you get is the meaning of the communication makes your job as a salesperson simpler. Consider the following analogy. My wife administers anesthesia. **She will only give you as much anesthesia as it takes.** She doesn't pay attention to the machines or any preconceived idea of what it should take to put you under. She keeps watching you and she keeps giving you anesthesia until you are "OUT," and she keeps you that way all the way through the operation. When the operation is through, she wakes you up. This is a real nice arrangement because it's not nice to wake up in the middle of your operation.

So, how much anesthesia does it take? **Just as much as it takes.** An alcoholic requires a whole lot more than someone who is sensitive to drugs and only needs a little bit. It is important to watch and adjust the anesthesia accordingly.

> **"There never were since the creation of the world, cases exactly parallel."**
> -Earl of Chesterfield

So, sensory acuity is the key to communicating just as it is the key to giving anesthesia. **How much do we vary our behavior until we get the response we want?** As much as it takes. The key to **Green Light Selling** is to be aware and to be flexible enough to change what you are doing.

STAGES OF A SALE

Your customer needs to go through a series of stages in their thinking process before they can make a valid decision to buy your product. Some customers go through many stages, others may only need to experience two or three. You should pay attention to which steps your customer has progressed through so that you don't cause them to skip steps and confuse themselves. Here are some of the steps most people enter at least briefly before they buy - the order may vary from person to person:

- SKEPTICISM
- CURIOSITY
- FEARFULNESS
- APPREHENSION
- INDIFFERENCE
- ENTHUIASM

Have you ever seen or been with a salesman that tries to keep your attention level at enthusiastic all the time? His theory is that you won't buy until you're enthusiastic. So **his outcome** is to make you *"enthusiastic all along the way."* What happens? He doesn't make the sale because you actually need to access a stage of curiosity or skepticism before entering a high-level enthusiasm stage.

Each stage your customer mentally goes through accesses a different part of their brain. Customer's usually have to go through more than two stages before they can make an informed decision.

130

Have you ever been wildly enthusiastic about a product from the first moment and after purchasing it became skeptical, apprehensive, fearful, and indifferent? You probably even suffered from BUYER'S REMORSE. Buyer's remorse occurs when the purchaser does not experience the various stages in their thinking process.

> **"He who findest fault, meaneth to buy."**
> -Thomas Fuller

So don't be disturbed when you observe your clients going through apparent mood shifts. They are working their way through the stages of their personal decision process. The **Green Light Selling** model is designed to allow your client to go through these various stages easily.

NEVER NEGOTIATE WITH YOURSELF IN FRONT OF THE CLIENT

Sometimes comments the client may make to you will throw you off guard. When you encounter a situation that requires internal self-negotiation, you need to somehow disengage from the situation or conversation and negotiate (even momentarily) in private. When you are asking yourself about the client's positive intent or feel irritated or offended by information offered by them, your first reaction will be to say to yourself, *"No way. Boy, are you ever wrong. How can you say a thing like that? Were you born on this planet?"*

Because you know to *maintain the right attitude (that they have a positive intention)*, you might have to struggle to convince yourself that their intent is positive. This conflict causes you to go into Internal Self-Negotiation.

Internal Self-Negotiation

So, here you are, absolutely and utterly convinced that this other person is trying to irritate you and is deliberately avoiding doing the right thing. Now you're going to convince yourself that is not the case, that they do in fact have a positive intention, and they're engaging in the best behavior available to them.

So how are you effectively going to disengage yourself and enter into an Internal Self-Negotiation, while the other party is right there?

The Approach

Somebody will bring up something that offends you and the first thing you want to say is, *"No way. How can you say a thing like that?"* And you get incensed.

Develop a habit that goes like this: say, *"Wow. I've never really thought about it that way. Just a moment."* Then, to have a graceful way of excusing yourself, literally turn your body away. For most people it is as if you've stepped into a privy and pulled the curtain. Your client will react like you've stepped into a voting booth. Have you ever noticed that when someone goes into a voting booth people kind of avert their eyes a little bit, even though the curtain is pulled? Nobody wants to stare. It's private.

Take just a moment while you negotiate with yourself, then come back and say, *"And, I can think about it this way as well. Can you?"*

PREQUALIFICATION

Because **Green Light Selling** techniques are so incredibly powerful, it is very important to pre-qualify your customers. Lack of a pre-qualification process or an inadequate system tends to be the Achilles heel of most salespeople. The **Green Light Selling** model creates an environment for producing on-going satisfied customers that are a source of a lucrative referral business.

With an inadequate pre-qualification process, you will attempt to sell to *clients that are either not interested or too hard to sell.* Investing a lot of time with the wrong clientele is expensive. Because your goal is to produce a relationship, spending your time with the wrong people is pointless.

Three Types Of Markets

Most marketplaces have at least three levels. You would have to have three different styles for dealing with all three markets. The **upper level** clients are so difficult to sell to that it's very, very expensive to market to them. The government or any funded agency usually fits into this category.

At the other end of the spectrum are the **lower level** clients. Generally, these folks just call in to order (there is no selling process involved). To appeal to this market hang a sign outside your business that says, "Stop by and pick up our stuff" or put an ad in the yellow pages. Also included in this lower category are customers that are too troublesome to work with. The **middle level** is yours. These are the clients who want you to take care of them.

It's really important to focus your attention on a particular market. If you describe your product or service as something almost everyone can use, you've failed to adequately define your marketplace. When your marketplace is too big, you cannot specialize. It's the element of *specialization* that makes you (as a salesperson) a valuable asset to the client.

You do have a choice in the sense that you can select a marketplace with clients you feel comfortable with. Analyze your market and say, *"Which clients do I work well with and enjoy serving?"* Carefully pinpoint customers that are really happy with you and continue sending you referrals, then go find more of those types of prospects. By carefully defining your target market, you can typically **win 85% of that marketplace.** That still leaves 15% for other salesmen.

Believing YOU Are The Best Choice

The main reason defining your market is essential is that you must be able to look in the mirror and say, "I am without question the best choice to those people. I am structured in such a way that there is no better choice than me in this marketplace." If you can honestly say that to yourself, then the **Green Light Selling** techniques will work for you. If you can't, they will not be as effective for you. Because at some point your client will say, *"Well, I'm entertaining a proposal from your competitor."* You must be able to say to them, *"You have misread your own requirements, I am your best choice."* If you've done your homework properly, you'll be telling them the truth. It may take your client a while to understand this because there may be a price differential, or a service differential, or a delivery differential.

Fly By Night Competition

Now, there may be others trying to compete in your defined marketplace with a lower price. Because they're in there with a lower price, they're not making the kind of profits to sustain their interests in your marketplace. The salesperson/client relationship will break eventually. That's why you must not let your customer buy from individuals who should be selling in another marketplace.

Explain to your customer, *"Yes, of course their price is lower, and the product and service they offer is precisely the same. That's because they don't understand this marketplace. To sell in this marketplace you have to price the way I do. I know this is true, because I plan to be in your marketplace for a long time. The competitor you are also considering will have to either get out of this marketplace or they will be forced out, because they just won't be able to make it. They can't make enough money. And you have to point these facts out powerfully.*

STACK AND FALL THROUGH

This simple marketplace planning procedure is well worth considering. The stack and fall through process assists you in identifying and appealing to a specific market. Because specializing is to your advantage, this process helps you to carefully analyze and define a small marketplace. In the process, you learn the language and understand how your product's benefits relate to the particular industry you plan to approach.

Say for example, you sell a container opener that could be used by hospitals, physician's groups, nursing homes, movie theaters, or restaurants. You will find that each one of these industries must be approached differently.

- **You need to appeal to each industry using different jargon and identifying how the specific benefits you offer fits their various needs.**

For example, if you're selling to both an institutional foods supplier and a proctologist and you use the word 'backend' in your conversation, you will get two completely different responses. The backend in institutional foods is the storage area for the kitchen. The proctologist thinks of the backend as being the front of his business. The focus of attention will be totally different for these two clients.

Knowing the specialized jargon of a specific market allows you to have greater rapport with the client. When you enter the scene already knowing something about the people you're talking to (including their little quirks of language and the way they think about things), you'll be able to sell more effectively. It doesn't matter what your product or service is or how it's priced; the rapport you achieve using the jargon will be much more powerful than the features and benefits of that product.

The Stack and Fall Through Process
Follow theses steps to implement the stack and fall through process for you:
1. Define a marketplace that you would like to penetrate and service exclusively.

2. Make a list of all the people that are in that market.

3. List all of the prospects in your territory from most important to least important in that marketplace.

4. Start by approaching the least important prospect on your list.

5. Go in and sell to this low man on the totem pole. Use every **Green Light Selling** technique that you have learned. You may feel ignorant at first, but give it your best shot. You will get your baseline information on his industry from this prospect. With this specific information on jargon, benefits, and how the industry runs, you'll be able to have a hold on the entire industry.

6. Your learning process will begin because the prospect will point out to you how unknowledgeable you are and how it is that you don't understand anything about "their" needs. And they will be right. (So keep your cool, and listen carefully.)

7. You cannot learn by a single example, you need at least one to two more examples to have a comparison. So begin approaching the next lowest prospect on your list.

8. Usually by the time you have worked with two or three companies on the bottom of your list, you'll eventually make a sale. By now you have spent time and money on this market and you are probably in a loss position. Continuing to stay and make sales only at the lower end of the market will not be profitable.

9. As soon as you make your first sale, immediately go to the top of your list. Make a call on the most prestigious

organization within your marketplace. If you are selling commercial real estate, go to the most prestigious building in the area. If you are in the medical trade, go to the most prestigious medical center, and so forth.

10. You will sell these people. These guys will be hard to sell but you will get the rest of the experience you need. About now you will be breaking even or be making a nominal profit.

11. Once you've sold to the top and bottom of your market, you've got the rest of the market bracketed for yourself. No one can say you're too small or too large to handle their requirements. So you begin at *the top of the fall through process, selling each prospect from top to bottom.* **You'll wind up dominating that entire marketplace.**

12. So while you're making the money off of the first market place, begin the fall through process again. Begin identifying another marketplace by starting at the bottom and learning the language and the wrinkles of another specialized area.

Persistence Pays
The hardest part of the stack and fall through process is that there is so much work involved. But once the system starts to pay off, it's real easy to get lazy and go, *"Oh, finally I have won my spurs and it will never end. This will last forever."* It has been wisely said, "And this, too, shall pass." And pass it will.

Many sales people have great peaks and valleys in their earnings. They experience a few months of feast and a few of famine. That's because they don't understand the last component of this stack and fall through process.

Expand your selling into other markets. Consider other non-traditional outlets for what you sell. By targeting other markets, you are buying yourself insurance. You may think that your product is not suitable for different industries. It really is! Begin by identifying a small part of this different population which exists and already wants your product. **Then go do an incredible job for them.**

NEVER SACRIFICE YOUR STRENGTHS

Throughout your sales interaction, maintain and enhance the rapport frames (Safety Zone, Personal Responsiveness, and Leveraged Outcome), the integrity of your pricing structure, and "relationship." Those are the areas that most salespeople sacrifice to get that "tough" sale. By selling out, you are throwing away your reputation and your most valuable tools for repeat business. Below are some examples of what you might say which would violate your strong points.

- Safely Zone: 'Well we'll just have to go over his head."
- Personal Responsiveness: "I don't care what you believe, we are the experts. You will be saved."
- Leveraged Outcome: "Look, you're trying to do the wrong thing in the first place."
- Integrity of our pricing structure: "It's negotiable."
- Relationship: "Well I think I can get this deal but they'll never let us in the door again."

Those are some of the things that sales people do on an on-going basis. The **Green Light Selling** model contains valuable tools that are worth maintaining. So at all times, remember to protect those with your life. You need to protect your rapport frames, and the relationship with your client.

- **Warning - Customers are Perishable.**

By guarding these elements, and following the **Green Light Selling** model, you'll not only have a customer, but a happy customer, a referring customer, a repeat customer, and someone who'll give you more business and teach you even better ways to sell to the industry you have chosen. The time you spend learning and practicing to use these techniques effectively are your best investment. Accept the challenge and you pave your own way to success. Good luck, turning your sales lights **GREEN!**

It's the job that's never started that takes longest to finish.
-J.R.R. Tolkien

INDEX

CPSIA information can be obtained at www.ICGtesting.com
Printed in the USA
BVOW02s0427190516

448557BV00009B/108/P